Kentucky Folk Architecture

Kentucky
Folk
Architecture

WILLIAM LYNWOOD MONTELL

and

MICHAEL LYNN MORSE

THE UNIVERSITY PRESS OF KENTUCKY

Scholarly publisher for the Commonwealth,
serving Bellarmine College, Berea College, Centre
College of Kentucky, Eastern Kentucky University,
The Filson Club, Georgetown College, Kentucky
Historical Society, Kentucky State University,
Morehead State University, Murray State University,
Northern Kentucky University, Transylvania University,
University of Kentucky, University of Louisville,
and Western Kentucky University.

Editorial and Sales Offices:
The University Press of Kentucky
663 South Limestone Street
Lexington, Kentucky 40508-4008

Library of Congress Cataloging-in-Publication Data
Montell, William Lynwood, 1931–
    Kentucky folk architecture / William Lynwood Montell and
Michael Lynn Morse.
        p.   cm.
    Originally published: 1976. With new preface.
    Includes bibliographical references.
    ISBN 0-8131-0843-8 (paper : alk. paper)
    1. Vernacular architecture—Kentucky. I. Morse, Michael
Lynn, 1944–   . II. Title.
NA730.K4M66   1995
720′.9769—dc20   95-31103

Contents

Preface to Paperback Edition   vii

1 / Folklife Research and the Culture
Landscape   1

2 / Folk Houses   8

3 / Construction Aspects   41

4 / Barns and Cribs   52

Epilogue   87

House and Barn Plans   89

Notes to the Reader   101

DEDICATED TO THE MEMORY OF
Chris Chapman
1871-1950
AND TO
Jim Harlan and John Holloway
MASTER FOLK BUILDERS
OF THAT SAME GENERATION

Preface to Paperback Edition

Folk or vernacular architecture may be defined as architecture built for local people, by local builders, using local building materials. Folk buildings, like folktales and folksongs, are expressions of traditional cultural patterns carried in one's memory instead of being committed to writing. They are learned by informal imitation rather than by formal instruction. R.W. Brunskill in his *Traditional Buildings of Britain* (1982) goes a bit further with the definition by observing that such architecture is traditional rather than academic in its inspiration, that knowledge of construction is passed along from one generation of builders to another by word of mouth and imitation, and that the end products accommodate the simple activities of ordinary people in village homes, on farms, and in small industrial enterprises.

Architectural historian William Pierson Jr. says much the same thing in *American Buildings and Their Architects* (1976) when he comments that rural builders in earlier times had access to architectural handbooks, but, unlike their more informed urban counterparts, they had no preconceived ideas about theories and styles. Nor were they pressed by an ambitious patron to imitate the style of the aristocracy. Folk or vernacular architecture, then, like dialects and speech of the common people, exhibits a remarkable degree of originality and is richly diverse.

Folk architecture is the result of design and construction created with thought and feeling rather than purely from utilitarian motives. The function of a house is shelter, but the form or style represents the owner's own preference. Architectural historian Vincent Scully summed up the modern skyline of Houston as nothing more than "bulbous chunks of rentable space"; that is, the buildings are there but the people are missing.

An interesting statistic reveals that in 1970 only 5 percent of the world's architecture was designed by blueprint architects. The remaining buildings were built by folk builders who obtained the patterns from their peers or ancestors. The end products provided for the occupants a sense of comfort and belonging, much like that described by Michael Ann Williams in *Homeplace* (1991), a book that examines continuity and change in the way people view and use the interiors of folk houses.

The field of folk architecture involves the study of both form and style. Architectural form refers to the configuration of a building that makes it immediately recognizable at any and all times by someone merely viewing it while driving past it. Architectural style, on the other hand, generally refers to aesthetic trims, facades, stained glass panels, and the like that are employed to make houses more attractive to passers-by. Architectural style is also the result of blueprint architecture, which moves it beyond the parameters of folk or vernacular structures into period or classical architecture.

Folk architecture in America is marked by rather distinctive regional differences, largely because of the nature of locally available building materials. By way of illustration, houses in New England, the South, the Midwest, and the Northwest are typically covered with clapboards or weatherboards. Fieldstones or other types of locally quarried stone lend regional distinctiveness to houses in western Pennsylvania, northern New Jersey, and the Hudson River Valley of New York. Adobe is used in the arid Southwest, and sod buildings dotted the Great Plains of Kansas and Nebraska during pioneer times and may still be spotted here and there by the careful observer.

Folk architecture is also determined by climate to a large extent. For example, old French architecture still found in portions of Missouri and along the French Gulf Coast of Louisiana was constructed with the first floor left open to allow for the flow of fresh air underneath the structure. Much of rural New England is marked by barns and houses that are connected to each other by means of an attached storage area. And the dogtrot house, characterized by an open breezeway, is found in much of the old Cotton Belt and in the Upper South as well. Folklorists, cultural geographers, and others are vitally concerned with these various architectural forms on the cultural landscape, along with the materials used in construction, for these are the facets that help to identify certain cultural areas and attributes.

The Kentucky builders who cut the trees, squared and notched the logs, sawed and mortised the timbers, and split the roof boards possessed an amazing amount of folklore about their tools and materials. They knew how dozens of kinds of Kentucky trees would respond to seasoning, why a dogwood mallet was suitable for striking a froe, and why that froe should be dull. They knew how to make the proper wrap for a broadax handle, why a square peg did its work best in a round hole, and what would cause a board to curl. In short, though they lacked modern power tools and materials, and though some could not even read or write, they were well equipped with traditional knowledge and skill. Part of that skill was the ability to recognize certain basic structure types and to produce them according to local need and out of materials locally available, making whatever modifications ingenuity and circumstances permitted.

Although students of folk architecture have abstracted and labeled basic building forms and designs, the folk themselves have contributed some of the terminology. The most basic enclosure—for instance, the crib or pen—is widely recognized in folk usage. Similarly, folk metaphor appears to have contributed both "saddlebag" and "dogtrot" as architectural terms. These are simply descriptive—saddling for two reasonably balanced containers side by side and joined by a middle segment; dogtrot for an open area through which dogs (or chickens or possums) can indeed trot. It would be an error, however, to set up a precise canon of types depending on folk usage, for the folk do not read architectural literature. They do not catalog or categorize, nor are they consistent in their usage.

In an effort to discern and label some of the diffusion and adaptations of building types in rural America, certain geographers and folklife experts have used terms not found in either the folk lexicon or the established literature of architectural history. A notable example is the coinage of the "I-house," most prominently used by Fred Kniffen and Henry Glassie but also widely recognized and adopted by others who see some independent evolution and distribution of house and barn types on the American frontier. Just as there is no "official" version of the ballad "Barbara Allen," so there is no "official" or ideal projection of the I-house. The term, as these experts have used it, refers to any of hundreds of folk structural expressions having in common a certain basic formulation of room distribution.

Since studies of such other kinds of folk expressions as songs, tales, and regional dialects often reveal regional distribution of inherited colonial and Old World traditions, one might expect to observe similar phenomena in the traditional material culture of regional America. Folk architecture affords the best example of such expression since houses and barns and other outbuildings serve the most pressing needs of settlement.

William Pierson Jr. carefully debunks the notion held by some architectural historians that folk or vernacular architecture filtered downward from high society to the masses. In discussing seventeenth- and eighteenth-century English architecture, Pierson observes that building at the folk level was entirely the work of local carpenters who did have access to contemporary architectural handbooks.

Scholars who take a positive approach to folk architecture like to refer to it by using such adjectives as common, ordinary, and everyday architecture. It is indeed common in a given place at a given time. The folk builder, then, who is usually a local tradesman, creates not so much what he personally thinks is best as what he knows or senses his customers will want. Folk architecture is thus a social statement, one that helps to define local values and preferences. It is possible to look at the local built environment—the translation into physical form of a group's needs, desires, values, and dreams—and understand the people who live there.

It is tradition that regulates or governs folk architectural construction. And tradition is the element that tells us what, when, and how to do something without stopping to question it. Amos Rapoport, in *House Form and Culture* (1969), offers three reasons why tradition as a regulator in vernacular construction has virtually disappeared in most cultures: (1) a large number of building types have emerged, many of which are too complex for a single builder to master and oversee; (2) a common, shared value system has been lost, replaced by building codes, regulations, and zoning codes; and (3) modern societies place too much emphasis on originality.

As stated previously, folk architecture was built for local people, by local people, using local materials. But the arrival of improved technology and mail-order houses after the Civil War altered the situation in this country. Local people were still in charge of construction, but local materials were not necessarily used in construction any longer. Thus in defining folk architecture, modern scholars need to allow for mail-order building kits and improved construction technology. Building kits that included the works—doors, windows, mantelpieces, ceiling joists, exterior boarding—were supplied by Sears Roebuck, Montgomery Ward, and Aladdin Industries of Bay City, Michigan, during the late nineteenth century. They were shipped by water but especially by means of the new railroad systems that by then reached into all parts of the country.

In that era architects, builders, and manufacturing companies also distributed pattern books for houses. An abundant supply of journals and magazines, all of which carried the latest styles of the day, appeared as well. Altogether, the building kits and publications were great democratizing agents in American society, bringing together social groups and cultures all over the country. These forces of standardization notwithstanding, local builders and owners could still manipulate the mail-order house kits to conform to local preferences. Thus the folk or vernacular process continued and is present in some instances even in the 1990s.

Some present-day scholars are concerned with function, value, and meaning, but there is still a pressing need to refine the architectural typologies that have been created. Warren Roberts of Indiana University states that one cannot generalize about architecture until the various forms and styles are analyzed. And Fred Kniffen realized the value of documenting the older structures on the cultural landscape. They are, he says, keys to diffusion, keys to understanding the movements of people from one place to another.

The documentation of the older folk architectural forms is critical at this time, as most older buildings, except for those in the Hispanic Southwest, are of wood construction—and wood decays! So many of those historic structures have either vanished from the cultural landscape or are standing in a state of decay and disrepair, often hidden from onlookers by mobile homes or aluminum barns and storage sheds of recent vintage.

The present study is designed to illuminate the types and myriad subtypes of folk houses and barns in Kentucky. The entire state was our laboratory when the fieldwork for this book was done, and we also traveled widely across the South and much of the Midwest looking for parallel examples of the houses, barns, and other material culture forms found in Kentucky. This book, however, is not designed to stress ideas concerning the origin and diffusion of styles in folk dwellings. Rather, it represents a detailed survey made possible only through painstaking fieldwork during the period 1963-1974. We were fully persuaded at that time and continue to feel that we viewed an example of every type of folk dwelling in Kentucky and the Upper South. Only the more common ones are included here, however, for this study is designed only to introduce the reader to the broad field of folk architecture.

1

FOLKLIFE RESEARCH AND THE CULTURE LANDSCAPE

Recent field investigations by folklorists and cultural geographers demonstrate that early settlement patterns in much of the eastern United States are reflected in the older buildings of the major folk regions, and that already it is possible to generalize on certain traditional building practices in New England, the Middle Atlantic states, the Tidewater South, the Appalachian South, and so on. It follows logically, then, that one can learn more about regional rural life styles across the years by cataloging and classifying architectural forms and attendant embellishments, including older deserted buildings which are often in advanced stages of decay.

In modern dwellings, such as the ranch houses found in suburban housing developments, folk architectural ideas and technology no longer dominate. Modern building methods and modern materials make today's carpenters and bricklayers practitioners of a fairly scientific calling. Architects and other specialists provide specific plans, heating and cooling technicians install the proper duct systems and electrical units, and a master builder oversees the project from beginning to end.

But for older dwellings on the culture landscape, whether dispersed across the rural countryside or situated in small county seat agglomerations, there were no blueprints, no materials lists, and no specifications other than the traditional formulae in the builder's head. The modern carpenter follows the blueprint with modern tools. The traditional builder followed the traditional plan with tools appropriate for his time and place.

The Historic American Building Survey dating from the 1930s and the Historic Preservation Act of 1966 have created public awareness of the value of the study and preservation of historic architectural forms. These measures did not come any too early, however. A wealth of knowledge about the pioneer settlers of the Upper South has been lost because most attempts, regardless of how well-intended they might have been, have been too little and too late. Except for pioneer restoration projects by the National Park Service, no genuine attempts have been made to preserve or document old houses and barns and other folk forms of the region or to index and catalog manners of living known and practiced by the early progenitors.

While one is inclined to romanticize the simple and unhurried life-styles which are slipping rapidly from the culture landscape onto the unwritten pages of history, he must nonetheless be a scientific observer and record and catalog accurately what now is, and analyze the social stimuli which are creating change on every hand, so that future students of folk culture can view in retrospect certain traditions in the process of alteration, mutation, and even total metamorphosis.

Fred Kniffen, a cultural geographer who pioneered in the study of regional house types, calling them keys to diffusion, stresses the important cultural ingredients possessed by folk dwellings. Kniffen persuasively contends for "a dedicated group of young workers who will with all deliberate haste survey the surviving evidence of the oldest occupance forms and patterns . . ." before time and degenerative processes take their toll.

This force of field workers will indeed have to move rapidly in dealing with older folk housing forms, for they are unchronicled and are overwhelmingly of wood construction. Without immediate field inventories and documentary photography directed at recording the location, character, function, and history of folk buildings, it will not be possible to move at a sufficiently rapid pace to stay even one step ahead of the processes of physical decay which take a heavy toll of the old structures each year.

Not only do the older wooden forms fall victim to the ravages of time, but they also become displaced by changing cultural demands and aesthetics and cease to function in the capacity for which they were originally built. Like an unwanted, aged member of the human family, a wooden building without a real purpose decays rapidly and presents a sad spectacle in its final days as a crumbling mass on the culture landscape. Many of the old dwellings in Kentucky have been salvaged and are now serving new secondary functions as livestock shelters, hay or grain depositories, or tobacco barns.

It is imperative that we record the life histories of these rural folk buildings. Not only do they reveal much of the history and culture of the region's past and tell us something of the occupants across the years, but they also help us to understand present concepts and characteristics of the local people and to underscore the forces of social and economic change which are apparent on every hand.

The bulk of Kentucky comprises a culture region with basically similar ideas and cultural elements. When there is such homogeneity within a culture region perhaps a more descriptive term for it is folk region, an area which has been defined by Richard M. Dorson in *American Folklore* as "a place where the people are wedded to the land, and the land holds memories. The people possess identity and ancestry and close family ties through continuous occupation of the same soil." Folk regions generally have been identified by their inner core components, but their outer margins have not been clearly drawn. A major problem in the study of such areas is defining the limits of regions and identifying the zones of transition where one region fuses with another and where cultural elements of both are present. Many solutions could be advanced toward identifying such folk entities, but any which excludes consideration of verbal folk traditions and traditional architectural forms will likely fall short of the mark. Thus, to understand fully the kaleidoscopic nature of the American culture landscape, it seems imperative to study the folk regions which are the component parts of regional cultures.

The task is monumental. The lines which distinguished one folk region from another were sufficiently clear until the folk streams were subdued and generally thrust into the mainstream of American agriculture, technology, and mass markets. The birth and development of folk cultures, accompanied by the regionalization of folk dwelling forms, was accomplished mainly during the period from 1790 to the Civil War. Folk buildings tended to evolve along fairly predictable lines if the process were shielded from exterior forces such as weekly magazines and newspapers and agricultural bulletins and rapid transit devices, all of which inundated the entire country by the end of the nineteenth century. Most of the architectural forms and embellishments in vogue between 1865 and 1900 developed because of national influences and trends rather than because of regional concepts. Some areas of the country, including much of Kentucky, clung rather tenaciously to traditional forms, as evidenced by the material relics on today's culture landscape. Thus between the Civil War and 1900 there developed along concurrent lines what might be termed folk and national traditions in architecture, both influenced to varying degrees by construction ideas which were dispersed rather quickly and widely across the nation

4

through such popular magazines as *Harper's Weekly,* *Godey's Lady's Book,* and the *Progressive Farmer* or other regional equivalents. National trends in architecture became firmly established everywhere in the country by 1900 and signaled the decline of folk dwellings, except in those communities where people treasured cultural stability more than social change.

Construction methods and materials and the uses of buildings tell us much of the cultural characteristics and economic aspirations and capabilities of the people of a given geographical area. Brick siding, for example, an asbestos veneer on low-cost housing, bespeaks tenant farmers, sharecroppers, and urban poor virtually without exception. Function and construction materials are both important, and they will be considered in context in appropriate places throughout the pages of this work. However, the third and most important element of folk architecture, form, is fundamental to a thorough understanding of folk architectural traditions. Any sound system of typology and cross-cultural classification must be based on form. It is the basic criterion in a typological analysis because it is the least changeable of a building's physical and cultural components. Building forms follow broad, rigid outlines which are basic in architectural character. Height and floor plans are primary characteristics. Stylish trim, porches, and additions follow more detailed outlines but are more or less ornamental in character. It is a simple matter to place a veneer of brick or aluminum siding on a frame structure. Changes in windows and doors can be accomplished, and porches and cornice trimmings may be added. Equally easy to accomplish is the task of changing the nature of a building's function from a human dwelling to a cattle shelter, from a stabling area to a tobacco barn, and so on. But it is virtually impossible to change the form of a square cabin with a rear shed addition into a rectangular cabin with an ell addition, or to change an English hay

5

barn into a transverse-crib structure. In all these instances form is the unchanging factor.

The factors at work in the folk mind which cause people to select one type of building over another are basically unknown. Perhaps it is aesthetic consideration; perhaps it is purely economical, or a matter of function, location, climate, or maybe combinations of these factors. And although there is a definite process of individual selectivity involved in the establishment of regional folk house types, tradition is nonetheless the major factor. Amos Rapoport makes a strong case that the preindustrial vernacular design process in folk architecture is one of models and adjustments or variations on the standard type. Tradition permits individual specimens to be modified, but not the type itself. Since ideas of all types move from one folk region to another, either by diffusion or by sporadic jumps, the relationship between migratory routes and folk building patterns can readily be established. It is a truism that a group of people will rely on time-honored folk traditions if there are no exterior forces to alter their cultural and social stability.

Some house types do get mislocated, so to speak, in the process of permanent human migration from one geographical area to another. For example, the New England salt box house was never built in abundance in Kentucky; nonetheless, it was here in a spotty pattern of distribution. In similar fashion, the nautical term "cuddy," used to denote the small space below the forecastle deck of a ship, somehow was transferred to a community in the northeastern portion of landlocked Metcalfe County, where it is currently used to name the small room or pantry at the end of the rear porch (see page 35). The Tidewater house was borrowed from the Atlantic coastal area and constructed in Kentucky but in very slim numbers indeed.

The log cabin, the saddlebag house, the double-pen house, and the dogtrot house all seem ideally suited to wooded frontier zones. They were easily constructed from native timber and served well the spirit of the raw, independent frontiersmen. Yet most of these historic house types have ancient parallels or prototypes in western and northwestern European countries. Rapoport adequately refutes the notion that primitive and preindustrial folk builders always use materials conveniently located and that the nature and quantity of local materials determine form. One example will suffice. Houses in the limestone areas of Kentucky are generally of timber, although both stone and timber are equally available. Tradition and folk selectivity, not building materials, must be the explanations for the frequent and prolonged appearances of these house types in Kentucky and the Upper South.

2

FOLK HOUSES

MANY AMERICANS of the late nineteenth century had personal memories of life in a little rustic log cabin which had been built as a new western frontier was invaded by land-hungry pioneers. Those people who could not testify personally to this sort of existence needed only to recall to mind the testimonies of parents and grandparents.

The log cabin in America originated with the Swedish settlers in Delaware during the first half of the seventeenth century. This form of building was also picked up by the Germans and Scotch-Irish and was disseminated all along the expanding western frontier. It was uniquely suited to meet the needs of the youthful and vigorous American nation which blossomed during the eighteenth and nineteenth centuries when the population moved westward in ever-increasing numbers. In its ultimate development, the log cabin became as much American as the James River of Virginia or the Bluegrass of Kentucky. It was a part of the American experience and a seedbed of the American dream.

Nowhere in the country was the geography more suited to the use of the log cabin than on the wooded landscape of Kentucky and the Upper South. Gilbert Imlay, who in 1793 published *A Topographical Description of the Western Territory of North America*, observed that in

Kentucky and other frontier areas "a log house is very soon erected. . . . Sometimes they are built of round logs entirely, covered with rived ash shingles, and the interstices slopped with clay, or lime and sand, to keep out the weather" (p. 134). Necessity, tradition, low income levels, and environmental resources all combined to introduce and nurture the practice of building log construction units. Early frontiersmen were unable to carry the types of tools necessary for the erection of frame houses, nor would they likely have been able to own those tools due to the general poverty of most pioneers. They constructed what were viewed as temporary dwellings, designed to be replaced later by more sophisticated houses. Log construction was phased out as quickly as possible in Kentucky, but in some portions of the state building with logs remained as the standard practice until World War I, and occasionally even after that.

Late eighteenth century examples, such as those in pioneer Harrodsburg, were erected of logs positioned horizontally in place and secured at the ends by some form of notching (Fig. 1). This cabin type served only the most basic needs for shelter, for it lacked window glass, and had no decorative trim. Puncheon floors were common, but some had no floor save the bare earth. Early chimneys were generally of wattle and daub construction, which consisted of stacked or woven rods of wood filled and covered with a claylike substance (Fig. 2). Roofs were of clapboard. The R. Ballard Thruston photograph collection, housed in the Filson Club Library, contains several relics reminiscent of that earlier era, especially in eastern Kentucky.

A cabin is by definition a one-room dwelling whose dimensions are square—for example, fourteen by fourteen feet or sixteen by sixteen feet—or slightly rectangular, such as sixteen by eighteen feet or sixteen by twenty feet. The room may be partitioned into two equal or unequal living units by the addition of a nonweight-bearing partition. There may be an upstairs area, but the

V Notching

Square Notching

Saddle Notching

Diamond Notching

Full Dovetail Notching

Half Dovetail Notching

Figure 1

total height is never more than a story-and-a-half. Frequently, there is an addition to the rear of the main cabin or cabin house which serves for cooking and dining purposes. The addition is generally rectangular—for example, twelve by eighteen feet—and contains a fireplace on the gable end.

There is a fireplace on one gable end of the original unit, and a small downstairs window may often be observed adjacent to the chimney. The upstairs (generally a loft) is ordinarily reached by a narrow, steep, boxed-in stairway located by the fireplace; but a ladder positioned vertically against the interior wall sometimes served the same function in early days. Occasionally, the ladder might be on the porch against the outside wall, but the outside ladder came into use mainly after Indians had left the Upper South.

Existent examples of one-level cabins are found mainly in southeastern and southcentral Kentucky. These cabins are distinguished by the lack of a well-defined loft or attic (Fig. 3). When an attic was constructed it was framed into the plate log just above the door.

Story-and-a-half cabins (Fig. 4) are differentiated from one-level varieties by a roomlike space upstairs capable of accommodating a bed. A narrow stairway connects the two levels. (A vertical ladder on the inside wall was commonly employed as the means of getting upstairs in the earliest examples.) The upper level is three or four logs in height, or approximately one-half as tall as the first level.

In most of the story-and-a-half structures there is no overhead ceiling to cover the exposed joists. In earlier days nails were driven into the joists and from these were hung beans, corn, pumpkin, and numerous other home-grown items to be dried for use during the winter.

There was a common practice before 1860 of building the roof longer than the cabin at the chimney end (Fig. 5). It is said that this traditional feature, known also among the Cherokees of western North Carolina, permitted

11

Figure 2. Lincoln's boyhood cabin home between New Haven and Hodgenville. Stick and clay chimneys supported by a log foundation were common on the Kentucky frontier. Note, also, the rocks placed diagonally between the logs to serve as a chinking base.

Figure 3. This southcentral Kentucky one-level cabin was erected about 1800. Note the broadax or adze marks, the half dovetail notching, and the lean-to rear appendage.

Figure 4. Frame story-and-a-half cabin with a board and batten exterior. Photographed in northeastern Kentucky.

Figure 5. The roof is designed to shield the chimney in this cabin.

primitive stick and clay chimneys to be sufficiently shielded from rain and snow to prevent the clay from softening and falling away from the woody portions of the chimney. With the clay gone, the wood would ignite and the entire structure might burn.

Later variants of the story-and-a-half cabin were covered with dressed planks commonly referred to as weatherboards. The latter were especially in vogue as exterior boarding came into wide usage between the Civil War and World War I. Sometime during that period logs ceased to be the primary materials in house construction. This changeover came to different parts of the South at different times, but it had come to most portions of Kentucky prior to 1900. Random examples of log or pole barns were built as late as 1945, however.

In the Reid's Chapel community of Taylor County, two miles north of Campbellsville, is an old rectangular log cabin with a rear shed addition. It was built about 1790 by a Phillips family who migrated to Kentucky from New England. During the Civil War the cabin was occupied by a woman and her two children; the husband and father was away at war. Legend has it that late in the afternoon on a hot summer day the woman was working in the cabin when she heard someone knock at the door. She was greeted by a strange man who informed her that he had come to spend the night. The woman was frightened, but she could not run because of her small children. She told the man that he could stay but that he first had to wash his feet. While he sat with his feet in a pan of water, the woman picked up a broadax, chopped the man in the back of the head, and killed him. Later two elderly brothers moved into the cabin, but neither of them would stay there by himself because they reported that the place was haunted by the ghost of the murdered man.

Only a person who romanticizes the past would claim that life in a small, crude log cabin was easy. It was pleasant perhaps to some who actually lived the experience; but easy, no. One Marion County man who was born in 1880 claims that during his childhood the family ran out of money and because of his father's illness with typhoid fever they had to move into an old log cabin. "We managed to get by," the man recalls, "but the main thing about the old cabin that scared me was the snakes. They would come out and hang by their tails from the bare rafters and look at us. They never did bother us, but we didn't stay there very long!"

During the present century the log cabin has become a relic on the culture landscape, an oddity like the covered bridge, the rail fence, or the water-powered grist mill. Most Kentuckians today are so far removed in their thoughts and physical surroundings from the homespun life-style of earlier generations that it is easy to overlook the reality and significance of the log cabin as a home.

The single-pen cabin is the basic unit of construction from which numerous folk house types and subsequent modifications sprang. Pioneer house builders found it rather easy to accommodate growing families by using the concept of double-breasting or stacking the original pen. Like their Old World ancestors, some added a room to the chimney end of the first unit; others preferred to attach the additional pen to the end opposite the chimney. Some stacked the pens and obtained two-story houses as a result.

Double-pen houses were much in vogue among the common folk of Kentucky through the years. Virtually none of these structures are being built today, but their numbers are still plentiful on the culture landscape as Kentucky enters the last quarter of the twentieth century. Regrettably, scholars from various academic disciplines do not always use a common terminology in identifying the various types of these double-pen houses. Folklorists are generally in agreement, however, and refer to them as the double-pen house, the dogtrot house, the saddlebag house, the tenant house (our own designation), and the central passage (hall and parlor) house. These are the terms we shall employ on the following pages. It should be kept in mind that all the types of double-pen houses have two rooms on the front of the house and are never more than a story-and-a-half tall. These are the two defensible characteristics.

The only one of the double-pen houses actually to employ the term double-pen house as the identifying label is achieved by placing two rooms end-to-end with a chimney located on one gable end (Fig. 6). (Seldom does more than one of the rooms contain a chimney.) There is usually an outside door for each of the rooms. The original cabin is predominantly of log construction, and later additions may be either log or board on frame. Sometimes, especially in later examples, both units are of frame construction.

The double-pen house type is found throughout Kentucky and the American South but the extant specimens are noticeably old, perhaps signifying the end of a popular folk house type which has no precise American or European antecedents. The double-pen house is most assuredly related to the European idea of increasing the size of a building by means of an end addition; but it appears to be primarily a product of the American westward movement, finding fruition among the poorer whites and black sharecroppers of the region.

The dogtrot house is constructed of two approximately square rooms which open onto a broad, central hallway open at both ends. A common roof covers the entire structure (Fig. 7). The open space is sometimes termed a hallway, breezeway, passage, dogrun, or possumtrot; but it is most generally called a dogtrot. Folklorists use the latter term. There is a chimney on each gable end built of locally quarried native stone. The dogtrot house as a house type should not be confused with a subtype of the two-story I house which also has an open breezeway.

The dogtrot house has a tripartite plan. Similar plans, in which two rooms are separated by a breezeway, are known throughout most of Europe. In most of these

Figure 6. Formative double-pen house. This southern Kentucky example was built in two installments. The left portion is older and is of log construction. Note the stove flue in the frame addition.

Figure 7. Dogtrot house. This southern Kentucky example was erected in 1886 as attested by a date carved in the chimney on the left.

instances, however, the dogtrot has been enclosed and serves as a room. As we now know it in Kentucky, the dogtrot house probably originated in Virginia. By 1820 it was fairly common in southeastern Tennessee through the influence of the central passage house described elsewhere. It is known in the mountains of eastern Kentucky, but it is far more common in central, western, and southern Kentucky, especially along the headwaters of the Barren and Green rivers. It is usually of log construction, infrequently of frame, but almost never of brick.

Although possible, it is not likely that the dogtrot house resulted when an additional room was erected a few feet away from the original cabin. Theoretically that is the way it happened, but a combination of fieldwork and library research indicates that both rooms of dogtrot houses were generally built at the same time. This is true even of those ancient structures with unfloored breezeways, such as the primitive example which stood for years in the Cedar Creek area of Hardin County, now a part of Fort Knox military reservation. (It should be kept in mind that once a new house type evolved from additions, complete houses could then be erected to embody all the additions.) Admittedly, there are a few known examples where the two log pens of the dogtrot house were constructed at separate times. Such was the case with the Thompson homeplace in the Pierce section of Green County. The first portion of that structure was erected in 1829 as a moderately square single-pen cabin. Later a rectangular cabin was added with a dogtrot between the two, and the roof of the addition was extended cantilever fashion across the breezeway to connect with the roof of the original unit. The Thompson house was razed in 1954.

Early unfloored examples of the dogtrot house were identical to double-crib log barns, except for the presence of chinked interstices and gable end chimneys. The affinity of these two folk structures illustrates how early builders drew upon the concept of the single pen as the basic unit of construction and then elaborated on it when necessity demanded. Function is often very significant in dictating the form of a building. Whether one is building a dogtrot house or weaving a basket, the design he seeks is generally best suited to cope with the natural environment. The open central corridor of the dogtrot house allows cool breezes to blow through the middle of the house during the hot summer months, which likely explains the popularity of this house type across the central South.

The dogtrot house (and other folk houses) may have a rear ell or T addition, usually comprising the kitchen and dining area, with an open breezeway between the addition and the main house (Fig. 8). The logs of the addition are usually not fitted into the logs of the original house. Such passages are occasionally referred to as dogtrots, but this application of the term is likely incorrect. True dogtrots appear to be associated only with the open space between the two front rooms.

The saddlebag house consists of two rooms built back to back against a large chimney serving fireplaces in both halves of the house (Fig. 9). The saddlebag principle may be utilized to construct a subtype of the two-story I house as well. The saddlebag house itself, however, is always of cabin height.

The central chimney of the saddlebag house is virtually always of native stone. Some folk call this house a double-fireplace house; some actually use the term saddlebag; others have no special name for it. Usually each of the two front rooms has a door opening to the front of the house. A number of saddlebag houses in Kentucky have a single door in the front center—this seems to be the oldest form. In such cases exposed chimney stones loom directly ahead as one enters the structure. Interior doors lead from this short, narrow hallway into the rooms located to the left and to the right. This hallway, and its companion space at the other side of the chimney, is made into closets, or a stairwell and a closet, in those structures

Figure 8. Single-pen log house with ell addition attached by means of a once-covered breezeway, sometimes erroneously referred to as a dogtrot.

Figure 9. Saddlebag house. This historic house type was once especially common throughout southcentral Kentucky. Note the extremely large central chimney.

possessing two front doors. When a stairway is in one or both of the main rooms, closets may occupy both sides of the chimney. If the two rooms are not connected by an internal doorway, the empty space adjacent to the chimney may serve as a storage area for kitchen equipment and garden tools.

A typical saddlebag house stands deserted in northcentral Monroe County between Rock Bridge and Sulphur Lick, an area settled mainly by east Tennesseans. It was built about 1820 by Jimmy Harlan and was occupied by five generations of Millers after George Frank Miller married Mary Harlan during the 1820s. The oldest part of the house is the right front. The left room was erected in the 1820s and a front porch was included. In 1880 the porch was torn away, and a T addition was added to the rear. The original cabin had an ash floor. "The boards," according to a longtime resident of the house, "washed like a biscuit board; so white!"

One of the last persons to occupy the Miller place was Vasco Miller, who had a tenant, Roscoe Fish. Their relationship spawned the following limerick during the late 1930s, when radios were still "wonder boxes":

> Roscoe
> went to Glasgow
> to get a Vasco
> a Philco
> Radio

The saddlebag house was the dominant early house in New England. Such houses were considered inferior, however, and were replaced by the Puritans as soon as possible. Saddlebag additions much like those found across Kentucky, save the Bluegrass where they were rare, were once common in the Tidewater and Piedmont regions of Virginia and North Carolina. The Watauga settlements of east Tennessee acted as a giant magnet and fan in attracting and disseminating saddlebag houses throughout most of Tennessee, Kentucky, the Deep

25

South, and into portions of Indiana, Illinois, and Missouri.

During the latter part of the nineteenth century and early years of the twentieth, the tenant house sprang up as a rather distinct adaptation of the saddlebag house. The tenant house, so named by one of the authors because of its widespread acceptance as a dwelling throughout the southern states for tenant farmers and sharecroppers, is a house type frequently found on much of Kentucky's culture landscape. It is generally a story-and-a-half tall, is almost always framed and covered with weatherboards, has two front doors, and possesses a small, central chimney which serves as a double flue for stoves located in each of the two front rooms (Fig. 10).

There appears to be a generic relationship between the tenant house type and the saddlebag house. Both have two front rooms and a central chimney. However, only the saddlebag house possesses fireplaces. The tenant house may spring from pioneer times, for two known tenant houses with stovepipe central chimneys—one in Taylor County and one in Adair County—predate the oldest remaining saddlebag houses known to us. Each of these has only one front door, unlike the typical two-door varieties of later years.

The two rooms across the front almost always function as a parlor and a guest bedroom. The kitchen and dining area are located in a rear addition; sleeping quarters are upstairs. Late nineteenth century examples were constructed with T or ell additions; but the more recent flimsy, "shack" variety of the tenant house contains a lean-to shed addition tacked onto the back of the structure.

The folk offer plausible reasons for the presence of two front doors in tenant houses and dwellings. One elderly gentleman volunteers this rationale: "There is one door straight back to where the kitchen is. By using wood to cook with in the summer, it gets hot. With two front doors, you can open one and it will make a draft for wind to blow

Figure 10. Tenant house. Houses like this one, especially with fewer square feet, are found across Kentucky. The central flue serves stoves instead of fireplaces. Photographed in eastern Kentucky.

through to make the kitchen cooler." Other people feel that the second door was present to aid the escape of family members should a fire break out. And one man claims that the second door was included to accommodate guests who were staying overnight. Should the visitor decide to "go outside and count the stars," i.e., go to the toilet, he would not have to announce his intentions to his host by making an exit through the parlor.

In scattered areas of the American South there are handsome one-story houses, of brick or frame, composed of two large rooms with an unusually broad enclosed central hallway between them containing a large doorway at each end. Such central passage houses evolved from the medieval English structure known as the hall and parlor house, which was characterized by two bays (rooms). The "hall" was actually a room as we know it. It was the first part of the house to be built and was larger than the parlor, which was added later.

The desire for more privacy and more living space led to the erection of a partition which created a central passage between the hall and the parlor. This is the central passage house (Fig. 11), the most common contemporary form of the older hall and parlor house found in Kentucky and elsewhere in the South. Some folklorists refer to this newer form as the hall and parlor house.

Central passage structures, many of which have heavy applications of gingerbread, have been observed throughout the commonwealth, although they are extremely scarce in the Appalachian region. With these Kentucky examples brick chimneys may be located externally on each gable end; they may be flush with the gable end; or, influenced by Greek Revival houses, they may be flush with the wall only to disappear into the building near the top and reappear on the ridgeline of the roof a foot or so in from the gable end (Fig. 11). In several examples, the fireplaces have been placed against the hallway walls, thus pairing the chimneys on the roof near

Figure 11. Central passage house. Photographed in western Kentucky. Note the flush chimneys which disappear into the second story and reappear on the ridgeline of the roof.

the center of the house. This arrangement changes the appearance of the house but not its essential tripartite format.

The two-story single-pen house, or one-room-over-one, is achieved by stacking a single-pen cabin atop a single-pen cabin (Fig. 12). An attic tops the second story. The large rooms are essentially square, and they may be partitioned with nonweight-bearing walls into two or three living areas.

Most of these old two-story houses present a tall, narrow front profile and may look somewhat off balance due to the rambling one-story ell or T addition at the rear. They are sturdily constructed, however, and are generally of log. As is the case with so many of Kentucky's folk houses, the weatherboard exterior belies the rustic nature of the original materials beneath.

The gable end chimney may be native stone, stone with a brick flue, or entirely brick. The door is almost always located in the front center, although it may be placed off-center; and infrequently it is found in the gable end opposite the chimney.

The two-story single-pen house was introduced by English settlers into the British colonies all along the coastal regions. From the Virginia Tidewater it diffused westward into the Piedmont, where frame examples may still be found. This house was also adopted by the Pennsylvania Dutch in southeastern Pennsylvania, and was carried westward from that point.

There appears to be no center of density in Kentucky for the two-story single-pen house. It can be observed infrequently in all sections of the state, and is among the oldest dwelling types here. The one-over-one concept in folk housing was generally not sufficient for growing families. Some of these structures were enlarged by means of a one-story addition to one side, which served as a kitchen. Others were expanded by building an adjacent

Figure 12. Two-story single-pen house in southern Kentucky. Note the door in the gable end.

one-over-one unit, thus exactly doubling the size of the original house. The resultant form was a house which looks like an I house.

In one of its many forms the I house, a two-story house which was borrowed directly from England, diffused westward from New England, and southward and westward from the Middle Atlantic states. It became popular in the Cotton South, the Upper South, the Ohio Valley, the Great Lakes area, and the Middle West. The I house was so named by Fred Kniffen in 1936 in recognition of the states of Indiana, Illinois, and Iowa, where it was most widely accepted and became the typical folk house.

The I house is two rooms wide, two rooms high, and one room deep. Beyond this constant feature there are no definitive characteristics of the I house, since there is no "official" form of the I house. Numerous subtypes of the I house are assigned on the basis of the placement of chimneys, the presence of a central hallway, and so on. End chimneys are more characteristic in Kentucky, but central chimneys are not at all uncommon. Ell, T, or rear shed additions are common, and porches across the front and side rear are usually present. The front of the house generally has one door and four or more windows. Large end windows are common in most I houses. Some varieties possess small windows on one or both sides of the gable end chimneys at the second level.

There is a form of the I house which might be termed a *two-story dogtrot*, although the breezeway, or dogtrot, occurs only on the first level. The bulk of the existent examples of this subtype are in southcentral Kentucky, and approximately two-thirds of them now have their breezeways enclosed. These houses are almost always constructed of logs which have since been covered with weatherboarding.

The *central hallway I house* (Fig. 13) is the typical southern I house. The inclusion of the central hallway represents a borrowing from the Georgian house. A chimney is generally a feature in each of the two front

Figure 13. Typical example of an I house with a central hallway. The end addition shown at left served as a physician's office. Photographed in the eastern Bluegrass.

rooms. Most of these chimneys are extremely large and are situated externally on the gable ends. The central hallway is present both downstairs and upstairs. These houses, some of log construction, are among the oldest in Kentucky. Weatherboarding covers the logs, however, except in extremely rare cases.

Central hallway I houses are occasionally found with the chimneys paired near the center of the house on the ridgeline of the roof (Fig. 14). Known examples containing paired chimneys, although 85 to 110 years old, are of frame construction. A rear appendage is almost always present.

Closely related to the I house subtype with twin chimneys paired on the ridgeline is a variant form which has one chimney situated either externally or internally on the gable end and another one located on the ridgeline of the roof just off center. Buildings conforming to this pattern are rare, however.

Houses containing a large chimney on one gable end only are infrequently found across Kentucky, but are more common along the western margin of the mountains. There are both log and frame examples, although the latter are more common. While no conclusive evidence can be presented, it appears that these houses evolved from two-story single-pen houses. One well-preserved Clinton County example grew from a log two-story single-pen house which was constructed about 1800. For the most part, however, *I houses with a single end chimney* (Fig. 15) were built in their entirety at one time.

I houses with a two-story portico were introduced into Kentucky at an early date. Construction of this type house flourished only between 1840 and 1890, however. The freestanding portico on I houses is generally designed to shelter the doors found at both levels, although it likely stems from Greek Revival influence. The roof of the portico may be gable shaped (Fig. 16) or it may be flat with a slight forward pitch. Because a central hallway is

34

Figure 14. Central hallway I house with chimneys paired on the ridge of the roof; located in the outer Bluegrass. Note the pantry or cuddy at the rear.

Figure 15. I house with single end chimney. Note the rather unique hip on each gable. Photographed in southern Kentucky.

Figure 16. This I house with two-story portico is so commonly found in the better farming areas of Kentucky that it virtually constitutes a separate I house subtype. It has a central hallway. Photographed in the Bluegrass.

present in these buildings, it would not be improper to designate this as a subtype of the central hallway house.

The two-story portico I house, described above, is typical of antebellum homes in the rural South, and examples built as late as the 1950s are still frequently found across the Deep South. They stem from slavery times in Kentucky and were much in vogue as houses for slaveholders who lived in the shadow of the Bluegrass and tried to emulate the aristocratic life-styles of the big planters in their Georgian and Greek Revival style houses.

The *I house with a central chimney* is the least common subtype of the I house in Kentucky and is equally scarce throughout the Upper South and the Midwest. Despite its spotty distribution, however, the central chimney structure is found in all areas occupied by other forms of the I house. Early examples of this house were found in such abundance in Puritan New England that some folklorists refer to it as the New England I house. The central chimney is of massive proportions in the earlier Kentucky examples and is made from native stone or brick. In such cases these I houses could just as easily be termed two-story saddlebag structures, for the "forked chimney" serves fireplaces in each of the two downstairs front rooms. In rare examples upstairs fireplaces also utilize the chimney.

In more recent examples of the central chimney I houses—roughly one-half of all those observed by us— the chimney is a brick flue only and accommodates tin stove pipes. The fireplace has been replaced by a cast-iron stove.

One of the least popular embellishments on I houses is the central Gothic gable on the front of the house. This feature which perhaps does not constitute a defensible subtype, is found on houses throughout Kentucky but never in abundance. The Gothic Revival occurred in the United States between 1840 and 1860 and challenged the

Figure 17. Gothic gables may be located on various house types, most notably I houses and double-pen houses. This double-pen structure may be mistaken for an I house because of the presence of the prominent Gothic gables.

popularity of the Greek Revival tradition. Gothic gables on I houses were a natural result of this rivalry and they seemingly should have received wider acceptance. The use of gables is a good illustration of folk selectivity in building choices.

Except for the Gothic gable, which sometimes closely approximates a dormer, these houses are otherwise choice examples of the two-story I house with single or double end chimneys. A few houses with dormerlike protrusions are found mainly in central Kentucky and thence southward into the counties of northcentral Tennessee. One, two, or three of these Gothic windows may be located on the front of the house (Fig. 17).

The *half I house* seems to be an appropriate name for the structure which superficially resembles one-half of an I house. Across the front of the structure are found the hallway and one large room. The half I house, which developed as a Georgian subtype, is a two-story dwelling. A large fireplace is located in the gable end of the front room, and, when an ell or T addition is attached to the rear of the house, there is usually a fireplace at the exterior end of this appendage. The half I house is fairly rare in Kentucky but has been observed in all areas of the state.

3

CONSTRUCTION ASPECTS

Nᴜᴍᴇʀᴏᴜѕ ꜰᴀᴍɪʟʏ ᴛʀᴀᴅɪᴛɪᴏɴѕ recount the days when
early Kentucky dwellings had no floors save the bare
earth. This was especially true of the kitchen if the cabin
home contained more than one room, which allowed the
privilege of a separate room for cooking.

In those initial years on the frontier before sawmills
were introduced, the most common floors were made out
of split logs, dressed and arranged to fit rather snugly with
the flat or split side exposed. These were called puncheon floors. Floors of thick wooden slabs, which were
smoothed with the foot adze, replaced puncheon floors.

As early as the 1790s in certain sections, and elsewhere
in the state by the 1820s, crude wind- and water-powered
sawmills were introduced and plank floors came to Kentucky and the Upper South. Most generally such floors
were constructed of yellow poplar planks because they
could be scrubbed with sand and shuck mops or lye soap
water and broom cane brooms, until the surface was
"shiny and sparkling clean," in the words of one person.
Another informant describes the cleaned floors as "so
pretty and white." Ash and oak planks also were used
extensively as floor timbers.

There were virtually no rugs in frontier cabin homes.
What few rugs existed were handcrafted. No padding was
used, except when occasionally corn shucks or straw

were placed under the rug before it was tacked to the floor to anchor it in place.

Log houses were nondesirable by 1800 in the larger settlements and even on the rural landscape when the owner could afford something different. Such possibility did not come to the common people of Kentucky, however, until the post-Civil War era.

When the logs were covered with shiplapped boards and painted, the result was an attractive building for family and passersby to admire that also provided extra protection from the weather. With the accessibility of clapboards (German-derived term) or weatherboards (English-derived term), it was no longer necessary to build houses with walls of solid logs. A framework could be erected of upright studs and horizontal timbers, then braced by diagonal members to form rigid triangular-patterned structural systems. Such a network of timbers was identical to the half-timber construction of medieval Europe and was derived from that concept.

It was customary to whitewash weatherboarded houses, rather than to paint them. Whitewash was made of slacked lime, which was derived from lime mixed with either water or buttermilk to a rather thick consistency. In that state it would adhere better to the boards.

Log houses and cabins were occasionally whitewashed or painted. "Burnt umber was used to serve the same purpose as paint," according to one source. "It was always mixed with raw linseed oil and came out red, brown, or black." Another source tells what the pioneers did with the old rough walls. "They obtained blue clay, of which there was an abundance in stream beds, and mixed it with water until it thinned down to paint thickness. They then would put it on their walls with rags because they didn't have paint brushes in the late 1700s."

Three chief fillers were employed to fill the interstices unavoidably left between the logs during construction: thin, flat slate or limestone rocks about 4 by 4 by ½ inch were placed diagonally into the opening; shingles of wood of similar sizes were used; or long poles or rails were trimmed to fit the empty spaces. Next came the chinking, a substance which was used to cover the fillers and to seal the crevices between the logs. Mortar was employed during the twentieth century for the most part to give a finished appearance. Earlier varieties of chinking consisted of a daubing substance made from mixtures of clay and hog's hair, clay and straw, or clay and small stones. All of these natural substances were abundantly available in Kentucky. Hog's hair was especially favored, for it was pliable yet long-lasting and prevented the clay from drying out and cracking.

Limestone or sandstone rocks, both hewn and unshaped, are the most popular means of supporting the foundation sills and girders in house and barn construction. These stones are usually stacked without mortar. Sometimes the stones number as many as six or seven in height, but generally only two or three are employed to raise the building to the desired elevation. Leveling the building also necessitates the use of foundation stones. That function has been replaced on occasion by concrete, which was introduced between 1875 and 1900, and by concrete blocks, which came into vogue about 1920.

Buildings were elevated to an aboveground position to prevent easy entry by snakes and rodents. Some structures, especially corn cribs, are perched atop four twenty-inch stones erected in vertical positions.

The roof is a basic need of mankind. It keeps out bitter cold and shelters humans and animals from the sun and weather. Shingles were commonly employed as roofing materials in England until the fourteenth century and were still in use there until recent times for church spires in the southeastern counties. They were eventually superseded by slate and tile. Wood shingles, which were hand-riven with a froe from good oak timber, were the traditional means by which Kentucky houses and barns, both large and small, were initially covered. Today very few folk buildings are covered with shingles (Fig. 18).

43

Figure 18. Jesse Gibbons nails wooden shingles on a house under reconstruction in the Hensley settlement, Bell County, 1974.

Perhaps each Kentucky county can claim less than two dozen such specimens on average, and almost all of these are in disuse and are decaying. Wood shingles in this part of the United States have been replaced almost exclusively by metal roofing or asbestos shingles.

Generally, the individual farm owner made his own shingles, also locally called boards and shakes. Apparently the process was not too difficult once a person had learned how to use the metal froe and wooden mallet. A lifelong resident of Metcalfe County described the process in 1965:

When a settler wanted a roof for his house or some of his outbuildings, him and two or three other men would go to the woods and select the best white oak tree they could find. (Later, they were made out of red oak and water oak or anything they could get ahold of.) They would saw or chop the tree down and cut it into lengths that they wanted for the board, usually two or three feet long.

They'd split it open in the middle, halve it, and work that down into bolts about four inches thin, take the heart out of it, and the width would be determined by the size of the tree.

They would take a froe—a metal, knife-like tool—and take the mallet which had been made out of a four-inch diameter hickory sapling. It was about fourteen inches long. And they trimmed the handle down for about ten inches, leaving a hammer on one end. You also needed a board break which was a fork made out of a forked dogwood tree, and it was cut off about ten or twelve feet long. They tied the fork end to a tree. Then you got two sticks about eight feet long and stuck them under the fork for legs to hold up the board break so it wouldn't scoot down the tree to the ground.

Then they had a wooden block about eighteen inches in diameter (cut from the trunk of the felled tree), and about twelve inches high to set the bolt of wood on. The froe was set in the middle of the bolt and struck with the mallet until the bolt was rived or split.

They proceeded to divide each bolt with a froe and mallet till it got down to the size of two boards or about one-half inch thick.

45

If the board started to split out, they turned it over and prized it with the froe until it came out like they wanted it to.

When they got the boards made, they cooped them up in small coops, or stacks, to season. After that, they were ready to roof their building.

The shingles or boards were smoothed down with a drawing knife. The seasoned shingles were put on the roof when the moon was full "or when it was growing." To put them on while the moon was dark or "shrinking" would cause them to curl up at the end, no matter how tightly they were pegged down. A Taylor countian relates the time his father put shingles on the house when the moon was shrinking. The birth of another son in the family delayed the father for a week until the moon was full. A pronounced difference in the color of the shingles could be observed thereafter, and those that had been put on first curled up during the winter months.

The fireplace was a constant part of all early folk houses in Kentucky. Lack of metal stoves on the frontier and lack of money with which to purchase them easily account for the prevalence of fireplaces. It was a simple and inexpensive matter to go into the fields and to nearby rock ledges to gather limestone or sandstone slabs of appropriate sizes for the construction of fireplace and hearth areas. Many creekbeds are underlain with natural strata of sandstone which may be pried up in four-inch slabs and chiseled into desired dimensions. These particular sources of stones supplied the materials for many chimneys constructed prior to 1900.

The fireplace was the focus of family life during those early years. The mother and father generally sat at the corners of the hearth nearest the fireplace. Almost always there was a window by the fireplace, although it was occasionally miniature in size. The mother occupied the corner nearest the window so that by the natural light she could see how to do her work, which was some form of needlecraft such as mending or knitting stockings for her family. Guests sat in front of the fireplace in the best chair the room had to offer—generally a rocker.

John Palmer penned an interesting description of the crudeness of Kentucky log houses, the hearth fire, and glassless windows in his *Journal of Travels in the United States*. . . (1818):

> The log houses are often miserable looking places, full of great chinks; if with windows, a hat, or a petticoat, is often stuck through the broken panes; paint is rarely seen. The fires are all made on the hearth. A fireplace . . . is almost unknown. All this is no indication of poverty, but an almost certain one that you will be received with hospitality; I have seen good looking brick houses, with the broken windows decorated with hats and petticoats. . . . It is a custom, originating in the difficulty in procuring glass, and the habit of procrastination, in which mankind are so apt to indulge (pp. 126–27).

A native Kentuckian reminisced about fireplace days during an interview in 1966:

> I can tell you about my grandfather and grandmother. They lived o'er in Adair County and they had a great big old fireplace in their house. This old fireplace was so big that they would bring in what they called a back log, and my grandfather would roll it into the house with big wooden sticks and roll it o'er to the fireplace and then put it up on these big stove irons.
>
> And then my grandmother would take a catalog or some old newspapers or something and make what they called lamp lights, just a twist of paper, and she would light her clay pipe. That woman would always be a-smokin' that there clay pipe.

The fireplace was more than a place for socializing or working or just resting. It was also the place where all the cooking was done in early days and where much of the cooking was done even in later times. A southern Kentuckian offered this descriptive testimony in 1964:

> When the weather was real cold, we would cook over the open fire. We hung what we called a dinner kettle over the blaze in

which we cooked vegetables and meats. We also baked bread and cakes in this kettle.

To cook breads we would put hot coals on top of the kettle; therefore, the bread would get brown on top. If you saw that the bread was getting brown too fast, you could take some of the coals off the top.

Many people think that this food was and is much better than modern-day cooking. Even today some people still use this primitive cooking habit.

A central Kentuckian recalled in 1965 that his mother did all her cooking in a "big old fireplace":

She had a big cast-iron container with a lid, called an oven. She used coals of fire under the oven and on top of the lid to bake things inside.

She used big black iron pots hung on an iron hook to boil food in. It was mine and my sister's job to get in bark to make good coals for cooking. This we did every day.

From various sources came recollections of roasting sweet potatoes in the fireplace ashes for a special treat on cold winter nights. Corn in the shuck, winter squash, and Irish potatoes were also roasted in the ashes during their respective harvest times. From the southeastern portion of the state comes this commentary on how to roast ears of green corn in the ashes:

The roasting of corn would come at about the last of August or the first of September. Build a fire and place the corn in the fire with the shucks on it. The shuck is still green and had to be roasted until the shuck was burned. The corn was supposed to be fairly done. Then take the remaining shuck off from it and go to gnawing. It was really done even though the corn was green.

Meat was also broiled over the hot fireplace coals. Another central Kentuckian explained in 1965 that it was necessary to have an iron rod extended across the fireplace. Ribs and other pieces of meat were suspended

48

from the rod and a skillet or similar container was placed under the meat to catch the meat drippings, which in turn were used for basting purposes.

Starting and maintaining a fire in the fireplace was a skill which had to be learned and perfected by two or more members of the family. This need was especially pressing during early times when stick matches were an unheard-of luxury. It is not surprising that the people of pre-Christian Europe venerated fire and came to look upon a fire's going out as an ill omen of serious proportions. This traditional belief lodged in the hill country of southern Kentucky. When the people were evacuated from the area soon to be inundated by the waters of Lake Cumberland, an old Clinton County resident reportedly made the Corps of Engineers move his log house and chimney in their entirety. It seems that the old fellow had a fire in his fireplace that had never been out since it was started more than a century earlier, and he was not about to vacate the premises and let the fire die out. While the house was being rebuilt, he remained faithfully by the old fireplace. Finally, the trucks came and hauled away the chimney stones. The old man rode on one of the trucks along with his fire and sufficient wood to keep it burning during the trip. When the chimney stones were restored at the new location, embers were carried from the truck to the rebuilt fireplace.

It was necessary to "save fire in the fireplace from breakfast until dinner, and from dinner until suppertime during the summer," according to a 1968 informant. "They'd put it back in the corner of the fireplace and cover it with ashes to keep it from going out. If it died out, they'd have to create a new fire. To do this, they would usually take and go to their neighbors and borrow fire."

If the fire went out at home, it could be rekindled by gathering a handful of kindling wood or wooden shavings and properly arranging them in a pile in the fireplace. Gunpowder was then sprinkled on the pile. Cotton could also be added to help create a favorable medium for fire. A gun loaded with powder only was then fired into the pile to ignite it. Indian flints were used in the absence of gunpowder.

An additional fire practice was brought to our attention. It seems that people, at least those in central Kentucky, would go to the newground at the onset of winter and start a stump burning. When in need of new fire, neighbors could go to the stump and get a chunk of fire to take home with them.

Many log houses would not stand the risk of letting a fire burn all night while the family slept. Life was by no means comfortable in most of these structures. A western Kentucky resident recalled that during his childhood in the 1880s the family lived in Breckinridge County in a one room log cabin. "The roof was so bad that when it snowed, the snow would fall on my bed. I'd just reach and pull the covers up over me. I didn't think much about it after awhile because I got used to it. The next morning when I woke up, the snow would be about two inches all over the bed and floor."

To warm the beds during the winter months the woman of the house would place bricks in the fireplace until they were hot. Then she wrapped them in heavy woolens and placed them at the foot of each bed. They kept the feet warm, and the bricks were still warm the next morning.

Frequently the traditional house is not the thing of beauty that the Kentucky housewife desires. She can do little to change the form and outward appearance of the dwelling. Her aspirations are often satisfied, however, by hard work and a sizable portion of folk aesthetic as the culture landscape around the house comes alive with shade trees, shrubs, flowering plants, rose bushes, and bird boxes attached to poles.

A handsome front yard with its cultured plants is a folk art form. Favorite plants include the needle and thread (Yucca plant), lilac, forsythia, rose, morning glory, honeysuckle, snowball, lily, and spirea, among many others. Numerous shade trees surround the house. This was especially true in the days before air conditioning when large trees were called upon to trap the wind and cool the area. Often numbered among shade trees are peach, cherry, pear, and apple trees, which serve the added function of bearing fruit for the family table.

A front yard covered with shrubbery and trees may indicate a bit of unneighborliness in some instances; it actually provides a safe zone where approaching visitors and travelers may be observed. Close friends and relatives might gather in the back or side yard, but strangers would be permitted in the front yard only.

Grass was not always considered necessary or even desirable, for that matter, when mowing would present a problem. Many yards in earlier times consisted of hard packed soil, and they were swept regularly with hand-fashioned brooms. Marble games and horseshoe pitching were favored forms of recreation in such yards.

The perimeter of the yard was enclosed by a fence in earlier years. The fence, generally of the picket (also called paling and slat) variety, prevented grazing and predator animals from entering the yard. Stone and rail fences were favored in some instances; but the white-washed pickets, held together with crisscrossed wire or nailed to horizontal braces, presented a neat and attractive appearance. Picket fences are relics on the culture landscape now and may be viewed only as parts of old deserted homeplaces which are engulfed by weeds and briars higher than one's head. Rail and stone fences, too, are falling into disuse and are crumbling in decay, except in those instances where they are intentionally preserved as rustic reminders of an era when times were not so fast.

4

BARNS AND CRIBS

UNLIKE HOUSES, which display various traditional structural motifs and embellishments, and songs, tales and beliefs, which have wide popular appeal, there is not generally a great deal about a barn to whet the aesthetic appetite, although some of us have a deep appreciation for their rugged and weatherworn appearance. If a barn type stands the test of time and enters the realm of the traditional, it is because the function served by this particular type has remained a constant factor in the geographical area where the barn enjoyed its greatest acceptance. An overspecialized function might even lead to a brief period of acceptance. One is not hard put to demonstrate that both the form and the function of certain barns have changed completely across the years. Some barns, such as the doorless tobacco barn, are rapidly disappearing from Kentucky's culture landscape. This particular tobacco barn was overspecialized and no longer exists except in mutated forms.

Despite the fact that barns surviving from early days are hard to find, the ideas behind barn forms in Kentucky can easily be traced back to pioneer days. That the old structures which remain stem from the architectural traditions of the late 1700s stands unquestioned, for the earlier methods of constructing folk buildings were uncontaminated by exterior forces until the 1920s. It was during that time that the United States Department of Agriculture (USDA) first offered barn patterns to Kentucky farmers through local county agricultural agents. Specific dimensions were suggested for hay and stock barns and new ideas were offered for the construction of tobacco barns. Only in the case of the latter structures were farmers receptive to innovations in their traditional barn patterns. The tobacco barn type which bears the imprint of agricultural publications can be detected readily, for the vertical distance from the ground to the ridgepole is much less than in older barns, and three driveways are characteristic. This is indeed a radical departure from the days when tobacco barns had no driveway at all.

Most of Kentucky's old barns and cribs will not be around much longer. They are built exclusively of wood and primarily of oak timber. Yellow poplar and chestnut may still be found in some of the more ancient structures, but these, too, are deteriorating from age and the processes of weathering. Soon they will be gone.

Among the surviving mementos of frontier society are tiny, log corn cribs which have been weakened by old age and are in the final stages of decay. Log cribs were seldom constructed in the state after 1900. They were easily translated into frame structures of a more contemporary nature, however. Now a common sight on the culture landscape are cribs, especially those with a central driveway, which were built of boards on a wooden frame. Field research indicates that some early cribs were used as granaries, mainly for wheat and rye, as is still the case with their European counterparts. In the main, however, these tiny structures were utilized for the storage of whole ears of corn.

Log cribs and certain log barns moved southward and westward from German Pennsylvania. Across the years, perhaps because of a southern location, the forms of these structures evolved along regular and predictable lines. Even functions of and attitudes toward the structures changed because of moderating climatic influences. Cribs grew smaller and smaller. From first serving as animal shelters they became more and more functional as cribs for the storage of grains. Cattle and hogs went largely without shelter in the American South. Hogs especially had to provide shelter for themselves. Tenacious folk beliefs tell us to observe the habits of hogs, notably sows, if we desire to know the weather in advance. (They will build crude shelters from limbs, poles, and leaves in advance of a severe cold spell.) Only horses and mules were sometimes stabled in lean-to sheds that flanked single cribs and barns.

There are several distinct crib subtypes observable on the culture landscape of Kentucky. Six of these may be identified for the sake of classification as plain cribs, cribs with a lean-to roof, cribs with a side driveway, double shed cribs, drive-in cribs—subtypes A and B—and front drive cribs.

Most plain cribs (Fig. 19) date from the 1780s in Kentucky. Most of these shelters, which are characterized by the absence of shed additions, measure about ten by twelve feet and have a forward projecting roof, derived from Appalachian ancestry, which shields the small front door from the weather. Rare elongated examples measuring about six by twenty feet have been spotted in south-central Kentucky.

A narrow windowlike slit in the side of the crib and up near the eave of the roof may be observed in some examples. This feature is not found commonly in cribs, however. It appears to be more characteristic of early doorless log tobacco barns. Some persons refer to cribs with this type of opening as side-loading cribs. Those with loading holes in front are conversely termed front-loaders.

The plain crib is often embellished by the addition of a low-rise lean-to shed which may serve as a hog shelter when properly enclosed. Sometimes the simple crib is constructed in much greater proportions of length, width,

Figure 19. Plain rectangular crib. Note the piled rock foundation. Photographed in the Hensley settlement in the extreme eastern portion of the state.

and height. In this extended form, the crib approximates a two-level structure in height. Such cribs are generally accompanied by a lean-to shed which is used to house farm machinery.

Cribs with a lean-to roof, or back-sloping roof, (Fig. 20) appear to be centered in westcentral Kentucky and adjacent areas of Tennessee. This roof form found its greatest function in the construction of outdoor toilets. Cribs with lean-to roofs generally measure eight by ten feet or ten by twelve feet. One noticeable exception, found in the eastern portion of Clinton County, measures eight by twenty-five feet; and a twenty by twenty feet example built in the late 1800s is located in Fountain Run in western Monroe County. While the exact age of the Clinton County specimen is not known, it contains a puncheon floor constructed of planks which were rived from logs.

Cribs with side driveway (Fig. 20) belong to a very old species, and some extant examples easily predate the Civil War. Log structures of this variety are no longer found in great numbers, but more recent examples of this type as board on frame innovations are far more common, especially in southern and westcentral Kentucky. Cribs with side driveways are characterized by a single rectangular pen and an open driveway. Each of these components has identical measurements and is covered by exactly one half of the roof. An enclosed lean-to shed may be added onto the pen side and used as cow stalls. The main pen, which is used as a granary or corn crib, is almost always entered through one end of the structure by means of a small crawl-through door. A door or loading slit may open into the driveway, allowing for ease of transferring grain or corn from the wagon to the crib. The driveway itself is generally used for storage of farm equipment. The driveway often served as a buggy shed in the preautomobile era. The usual size of the crib-shed combination is twelve by eighteen feet.

Double-shed cribs have two sheds displaying perfect

56

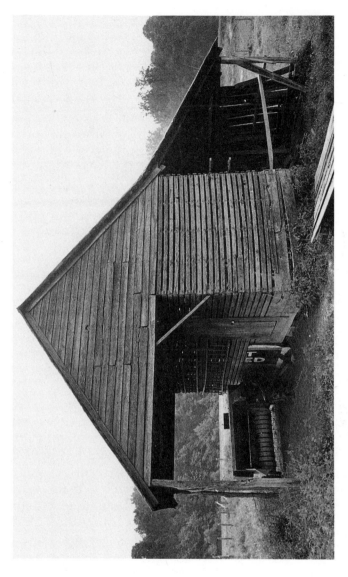

Figure 20. Crib with side driveway. Photographed in northeastern Kentucky. The lean-to shed attached at the right does not alter the basic type of the structure.

symmetry. They are even more scarce than the single-shed variety. While the double-shed crib might be classified as a subtype of the single-shed variety, such is not really the case. Lacking one of the sheds, the double-shed structure would have the appearance of being only a log pen with a lean-to shed. In the double-shed type, the rectangular pen is symmetrically balanced under the ridgeline of the roof. A cantilevered plate log forms the top log of the pen at the end of the building, then extends across the breadth of the structure to form the basic support for each of the sheds (Fig. 21). Typical dimensions for the sheds are eight by eighteen feet.

The double-shed type is fairly common to the Middle South, but very few examples of it were found in Kentucky. One of these relics stands near the banks of the Cumberland River in the Vernon community of Monroe County. An ancient log tobacco barn is located nearby, at the point where the fertile river bottom is terminated abruptly by the rugged Meshack Hills. Other examples of double-shed cribs are found in the mountains of eastern Kentucky, centered in Knox and Bell counties. The central crib in these examples is narrow and elongated, and the sheds may not be enclosed.

Drive-in cribs (Fig. 22), another subtype, are too large to be termed cribs and too small to be barns. Cribs of the type A variety are distinguished by two rectangular cribs measuring about five by twenty feet, aligned with the ridgeline of the roof and separated by a driveway. An upper level may be present. When such is the case, the second floor is a granary and is floored and lined with thin planks to prevent small grains from sifting through the cracks. Drive-in cribs are never used as stabling areas, but lean-to sheds, with dimensions of about ten by twenty feet, which shelter livestock may be attached. Even when stables are provided in this manner, the drive-in crib is still not the only barnlike structure on a farm. This enlarged crib structure is almost always used as a cow barn and may be referred to by that name. Horses and mules

Figure 21. Double-shed crib. This form is rather common in southeastern Kentucky. It does not have the cantilevered roof which is so typical of this crib type in other parts of the South.

Figure 22. Drive-in crib, type A. The cribs are elongated parallel with the ridgeline of the roof. Photographed in the Bluegrass.

are housed in much larger barns when family finances permit their construction.

Type B of the drive-in variety is characterized by two rectangular cribs measuring about ten by sixteen feet which are arranged transversely to the ridgeline. This crib is smaller than type A, seldom has an upper-floor granary, and is never converted into stabling quarters, not even through the use of lean-to appendages. Examples of type B are scattered across Kentucky, but they seem to be centered in the more rugged upland areas of the state.

Front drive cribs are characterized by a forward-projecting roof, which is supported by front posts and is sufficient to serve as an awning for a wagon or farm equipment (Fig. 23). Known examples of this small crib subtype are found in Clinton and Cumberland counties.

The ubiquitous log single-crib barn is frequently covered with a great sweeping roof that adds a shed on either side of the large single log pen, thus producing an end-opening barn. The sheds may be further partitioned into livestock stabling areas (Fig. 24). Some of these old structures are moderately rectangular, about sixteen by twenty feet, while others are built on the square, with dimensions measuring anywhere from sixteen by sixteen feet to thirty by thirty feet. The height reaches upward to thirty feet.

The single-crib barn is not only functional but also adaptable. Some variation of this barn was the dominant barn type of Kentucky and the Upper South a few years ago. Although the primary function is directed toward livestock feeding purposes, the single-crib barn, when the loft is absent, often serves as a tobacco barn and tool storage area. When a loft is present, the first floor is used to store corn and sometimes to house livestock. The second floor houses hay and fodder (and small grains if the walls are lined with planks).

The log single-crib barn is locally referred to as a "log pen barn." One Taylor County resident claims that "the

Figure 23. Front drive crib located in the Lake Cumberland area.

Figure 24. Single-crib barn located in southern Kentucky. The driveway and central pen are flanked by stabling areas.

old log pen barn" was the common barn of its day. "Back when timber was plentiful, the farmer built a big log pen. The pen served every purpose. He might have hay stacked in there, and maybe a corner fenced off for corn. Sometimes, even, he kept a cow or two in the pen. The sheds weren't necessarily built at first. They could be added on as soon as the farmer needed more room."

Many existent log pen barns superficially resemble frame barns when viewed only from the outside. A closer look, however, reveals the lack of a central driveway. On the inside is a log pen that is often surrounded on all sides by a driveway which is hidden from the outside by the exterior boarding.

That the primary function of the single-crib barn is to house and feed livestock is borne out not only by oral testimonies but also by archeological evidences. Hay mangers, corn holes, and hollowed-out log troughs are still to be found as mute testimony of the earliest function. A beech log thirty feet in length and containing a hollowed-out trough some twenty-four inches deep may be viewed in a log barn located along the banks of Indian Creek in Fentress County, Tennessee. Many log pen barns are used as tobacco barns today, except that one or more of the appended driveways may be used for cattle shelter as well.

Located in the southeastern region of Kentucky are examples of single- and double-crib barns whose large frame lofts overhang on all sides by means of the cantilevered principle. Because of the present scarcity of this type, it is apparent that such barns were never commonly found in Kentucky. They are especially prominent, however, in the Cades Cove area of the Great Smoky Mountains National Park and in adjacent areas. Similar barns were known in German Pennsylvania and are generically related to a medieval Germanic peasant house whose first story served as warm quarters for the family and whose second level overhung by means of the cantilevered process.

A Sevier County, Tennessee, example photographed in 1971 and reputedly dating from about 1800, has a large root and fruit cellar extending beneath one of the log pens and under the floored driveway. The cellar is entered from the barn's gable end. Other barns with a cellar were observed in the Maggie Valley area of western North Carolina.

Double-crib log structures are fairly rare on Kentucky's culture landscape today, but they were once very common sights. Although some of these barns were built during the 1940s, most of the existent examples predate 1900 and even 1880. These structures, which resemble dogtrot houses, have European antecedents, but they found a home among the early Pennsylvania Germans and other pioneers on the western frontier. All examples have disappeared from German Pennsylvania, but some may still be observed in the Midwest, Upper South, and Cotton States. They were especially attractive to the people of the Upland South and appear mainly to have survived in those areas where modern technology was slow in developing.

All double-crib barns are composed of two log pens measuring about twelve by ten to twelve by sixteen feet, which are separated by an open driveway or runway extending from side to side in the European fashion and connected by a common roof. The double-crib log barn can be grouped into subtypes in accordance with the parallel or perpendicular position of the log pens in relation to the ridgeline of the roof.

The subtype A barn can be distinguished by its two rectangular log pens which run parallel with the ridgeline of the roof. Although the stable doors may be located in the gable ends of the barn, they most commonly open into the driveway. There are no doors which close off the driveway, except when the double-crib barn functions as a tobacco barn. Tobacco barns of this type were once very common in the burley producing areas of southcentral Kentucky and northcentral Tennessee.

65

The existent barns of this double-crib variety appear in every part of the state; but they are mainly found in the mountains, in the Cumberland River counties of Monroe, Cumberland, and Clinton, and in the western Kentucky coal field. It might be noted that barns of this type found very little acceptance when translated into frame structures. They could not compete with the transverse-crib structures which were easily able to make the switch from log to frame.

Subtypes B and C have rectangular cribs which are situated perpendicular to the ridgeline and parallel with a side-to-side driveway (Fig. 25). Although common in the Kentucky mountains around Manchester and Hazard and in the area between Tompkinsville and Somerset, subtype B is fairly scarce elsewhere across the state. In log examples one of the cribs may be considerably smaller than the other, thus serving as a corn crib. The larger of the two units serves as a stabling area for cows.

In some cases weight-bearing partitions divide the two basic cribs into three stables or into two stables and a corn storage bin. These weight-bearing walls which divide the cribs are the chief distinguishing agents of the double-crib barn subtype C. Cribs without such interior walls comprise subtype B. When interior log walls are present the hayloft is always rather large. In a unique example of subtype C, found near the Vernon community in Monroe County, the three stables on one side of the driveway are of log construction, while the companion areas across the driveway are of frame construction. Yet the barn was built as a single unit, for the plate logs extended all the way along the eaves of the barn from one gable end of the structure to the other, tying the log and frame units together.

The double-crib barn subtype B may stem from the same archetype as the English hay barn, for their forms seem closely connected by the use of the side-to-side driveway. The double-crib barn in all varieties was as

Figure 25. Double-crib barn, subtype B. The yellow poplar log pens are arranged transverse with the ridgeline. Photographed in southern Kentucky.

much at home here in Kentucky as it was in its original homeland in northern and central Europe.

In its present form the four-crib barn probably originated in southeastern Tennessee along the Tennessee River. Of simple construction, these barns are composed of four single log pens, usually used for stabling purposes, separated by driveways extending from gable end to gable end and from side to side (Fig. 26). The earliest form of these barns consisted of rectangular cribs measuring about ten by ten feet and possessing docrs which usually opened into each driveway. More recent barns of this type are composed of pens which are virtually square, driveways of equal width, and doors which open into the gable-to-gable driveway. The side-to-side driveway has generally been converted into additional stabling areas by boxing it in with planks. This enclosure procedure led to the creation of the transverse-crib barn, described elsewhere. Some barns that now function as transverse-crib barns are actually converted four-crib structures.

Four-crib barns are seldom found on today's culture landscape in Kentucky, and then only in log form. There is no evidence that the four-crib idea carried over into frame construction, at least as four-crib barns. Judging from extant structures, the historic center of concentration appears to have been focused on the Tennessee hill country along the Cumberland and Obey rivers. Clinton, Cumberland, and Monroe counties in Kentucky have several examples of this barn type, and one is located in northern Warren County. Every known example is crumbling in decay.

The four-crib barn and the drive-in corn crib may be jointly responsible for the development of the transverse-crib barn, a structure which is the most common barn variety found in Kentucky and the Upper South. The core territory of the transverse-crib barn in Kentucky appears to be enclosed by a line drawn through Bardstown, La

Figure 26. Four-crib barn. Photographed in western Kentucky.

Grange, Campton, London, Cave City, and Elizabeth-town. The Bluegrass region has an especially heavy concentration of the transverse structures.

The creation of this barn was made possible by boarding up the side-to-side driveway of the four-crib barn. This step most likely occurred in the Great Valley of eastern Tennessee. A log barn found near Rock Bridge in Monroe County which was built by pioneer migrants from Johnson City, Tennessee, is a mutant between the four-crib and transverse-crib types. This structure contains one long, unpartitioned crib which extends from one gable end to the other, and two log pens which are separated by a short driveway. A regular end-to-end driveway is also present. The resultant driveway pattern is a T.

The exterior of the transverse-crib barn superficially resembles the drive-in crib, but internally there are fundamental differences of style and function. While the drive-in crib is a single construction unit and is used for the storage of corn or other small grain, the transverse-crib barn is divided into two or more stabling areas of twenty to fifty feet length on each side of the driveway. The stabling areas are usually divided at eight or ten foot intervals to produce individual stables. Generally, a portion of one of the stabling areas is set aside for the storage of corn or small grain or for gear space. The oldest examples of the transverse-crib barn are log, but at an early date boards over a log frame won widespread usage. By 1900 the transverse-crib barn was the most common type of barn seen on Kentucky's landscape. Wing-type shed additions did not change the basic style (Fig. 27). Thus many of the transverse-crib structures found in northern Kentucky, in the Bluegrass region, and between Eliza-bethtown and Leitchfield, are actually wing-shaped. While a pseudo-hay hole may be present in the front gable end, hay was (or is) most usually tossed by pitchforks into the second story from wagons which were pulled into the driveway. The wing-type sheds are gener-

Figure 27. Transverse-crib barn with wing sheds. Photographed in western Kentucky. The middle driveway is flanked by stabling areas.

ally poor for hay storage, but they are excellent tool and machine sheds. Because of this utility wing-shed barns won wide acceptance in the big ranch country of the southwestern United States.

Although smaller transverse-crib barns are still being built, they have given way in popularity to large stock barns and feeder barns with their characteristic massive hay holes and track-mounted hay forks. These comprise subtypes of the transverse-crib barn.

The large stock barn subtype is easily recognized when observed on the landscape because of its gigantic size and multiple driveways—generally three and sometimes five. This is not strictly a barn type, however, since it lacks definite distinctive form and cannot be subclassified according to layout. The large stock barn is found in central Ohio and in the more prosperous farming areas of Kentucky and Tennessee, especially in the Bluegrass and Nashville basins, and on almost all of the fertile creek and river bottom farms in the other areas of both states, where it is possible to approximate a midwestern farming economy.

The large stock barn had its origin as early as the 1880s; but it did not win wide acceptance until the 1940s, when farmers could afford the luxury of the hay fork and pulley and rope method of storing hay in the spacious loft. The rope, which was secured to the fork, ran across the inside top of the barn and out the back end, where it was tied to a horse. As the animal walked away from the barn, the fork lifted the hay from the wagon to the ridgeline of the barn where a metal track carried the hay to the desired spot. At that point, the men reached out, grabbed the hay, and stacked it in position. The process was then repeated. Advanced mechanization methods have altered this procedure of unloading the hay, but they draw heavily upon the earlier ideas.

A forward projection of the roof, which shelters the metal track of the hay fork, can be seen on most of the large stock barns (Fig. 28). The blunt or square end

Figure 28. Transverse-crib barn with hanging gable. Photographed in central Kentucky.

examples may be a product of USDA influence, but the pointed projections date to the pre-Civil War period. The latter projections are referred to as "hanging gables," since they have the appearance of "hanging without support." This feature, also observed on many barns in central Ohio, is called a "bonnet" in some parts of Michigan. Barns with hanging gables are common on the Springfield Plateau and extend into eastern Oklahoma.

The feeder barn subtype, also called a stock barn or hip barn, is rigidly centered geographically in Barren and Metcalfe counties. Its area of distribution extends only a few miles into the adjoining counties and there stops abruptly. The feeder barn, derived from the transverse-crib barn, may vary slightly from the latter in layout, especially when additional sheds are attached. But the basic plan consists of a central driveway flanked by a row of stables, measuring about seven by eight feet, on either side. One or two of the stables may be set aside as gear rooms or corn cribs. It is generally from these rooms that stairways lead to a massive hay loft. Sometimes the loft is entered by a ladder from the driveway or, more frequently, from a catwalk or narrow passageway which extends lengthwise of the barn between the driveway and the feeding area.

The feeder barn is differentiated from the large stock barn by means of an inward slope of the outer walls about one-third of the way from the ground to the roof (Fig. 29). One or both walls may be so constructed. Farmers who build this barn claim that the indented walls allow a higher degree of manger space utilization. Because of this claim regarding function, one is led to suspect that the feeder barn is the product of early USDA publications. The writers have been assured by county agricultural agents that such is not the case, however. C. V. Bryan, retired agent for Taylor County, told us that USDA barn patterns first came to the eastern Pennyroyal in about 1920. A Monroe countian additionally placed the origin of this barn type during an earlier period. He could trace

74

Figure 29. Hip barn with ground-level gable entrance into the second story. Photographed in westcentral Kentucky.

construction of a Monroe County specimen to the 1880s. And an elderly lady in the northern part of Barren County noted that she had "seen these barns all her life."

One of the most uncommon barn types in the state is the English or Connecticut barn. This barn is widely known in Europe, especially in England, Scotland, and Germany, where it contains a threshing floor in lieu of the driveway. It was carried to America by early immigrants and diffused westward from such focal points as Puritan New England, southeastern Pennsylvania, and the Tidewater and Piedmont areas of the South Atlantic states. It then entered Kentucky during the earliest days of settlement but was not widely accepted. Today the examples on the landscape are derived mainly from New England and are all of frame construction. Two of these barns with relic threshing floors were located in the Hickory College section of Metcalfe County until recent times. Built about the time of the Civil War, the floors in these barns sloped downward to the center where a slit permitted grains to sift into a container under the floor. Flailing sticks were employed to separate the grains from the chaff.

The English barn is composed of two stabling areas measuring about nine by twenty-four feet located across the driveway from each other (Fig. 30); consequently, there is a close affinity to subtype B of the log double-crib barn. The driveway of the hay barn extends through the center of the barn from side to side rather than from end to end, as is the case with transverse-crib barns. There is an open hay loft at the second level on each side. The driveway is generally closed off at both ends by large double doors, while smaller doors lead from the driveway into the livestock stables.

It is not at all uncommon in Kentucky for the English barn to be totally void of stabling areas, corn crib, and hay loft, and filled instead with an orderly arrangement of tier poles for the storage of tobacco. An identical function is served by this barn in the tobacco producing areas of eastern Maryland and Virginia.

Figure 30. English barn. This example was photographed in eastern Kentucky, where it is very rare. Barns of this type are more commonly found in northern and central Kentucky.

Occasionally the English barn may be built against a bank designed to provide a side entry at ground level into the loft area of the barn. The access ramp may be elevated at the proper angle by making a rock or concrete fill or by literally positioning the barn against a mound of earth, thus making a natural entrance to the second level a reality.

The loft is a spacious area designed solely for the storage of hay. The expanse is broken only by support posts interspersed throughout, by a grain bin located in one corner only, and by hay holes which permit hay to be tossed into the mangers below. Horse- or tractor-drawn wagons can easily be pulled in and out of the loft area.

The first level, or "basement" level, of the bank barn is structured exactly like a transverse-crib barn; i.e., the driveway runs from gable end to gable end and there are stabling areas forty to fifty feet long on each side of the driveway. Generally, there is a lean-to shed on the side farthest away from the loft entrance.

The bank barn is rather large in overall dimensions. Because of its size, coupled with the side entrance, plus the fact that an overhanging forebay may sometimes replace the lean-to shed addition, one is led to conclude that Pennsylvania Dutch influences may have been stronger than those of the English hay barn in creating the bank barn subtype.

Although bank barns are rather common in central and southeastern Ohio, some even having Gothic gables, these structures are generally scarce in Kentucky. They appear to be centered in the triangular area between Louisville, Lexington, and Greensburg. Even in this area only widely scattered examples can be spotted. Virtually all of them are in good condition, a factor which indicates a fairly recent origin or a high degree of functionality.

Cow barns, like tobacco barns, cannot be classified along typological lines. Older farmsteads commonly boasted a structure which served as a cow barn (milking

parlor in modern terminology). The cow barn had stabling areas, a hay loft, a corn crib, and even a granary in
many instances (Fig. 31).

Almost all of the cribs and barns already described in
this study may occasionally function as tobacco barns.
Verging on the point of absurdity, for example, was the
Adair County corn crib which measured only six by eight
feet but was filled with sticks of spiked tobacco during the
fall of 1967.

There is no single barn type in the Kentucky-Ten-
nessee burley belt which may truly be called a tobacco
barn. One of the common varieties, found in central and
southcentral Kentucky, is nothing more than an English
hay barn stripped of its insides and replaced by a lattice of
horizontal beams (tier poles) spaced about four feet apart.
Another form, basically akin to the transverse-crib barn,
which is known throughout the entire Upper South and
especially common in the Cumberland River country, is
the barn pictured in figure 32. It serves both as tobacco
barn and stock barn. The two functions are seldom mixed
under the same roof, however. The ventilator found along
the peak of the roof is the most distinctive feature of this
type of tobacco barn. Older forms of the pictured ventilator are of the same width but four to six feet taller,
while the most recent form of the ventilator is far more
narrow than the earlier forms.

The nearest approach to a tobacco barn type is shown in
figure 33. It represents the last folk creation in tobacco
barns before the advent of the three-driveway structures
suggested by publications issued by the USDA during
the 1920s. This barn is always used as a tobacco barn, but
it is situated close enough to the livestock barns that it can
serve as a shelter for feeder cattle during the winter
months. If any tobacco barn could be termed typical of the
burley tobacco barn, this is it. Like most tobacco barns of
the area, this type is seldom painted. Very few farmers in
earlier years could afford the luxury of paint. For those

79

who used paint, red was the predominant color choice at one time; but black is the popular choice in recent years.

Ancient tobacco barns had a long slit—generally a missing log—in one side of the structure. Oldtimers claim that the slit was a hole through which sticks of tobacco were handed to workers on the inside. Although there are no known extant examples, there is strong oral tradition in southcentral Kentucky which claims that pioneer tobacco barns were built as doorless and windowless log pens, except for the opening in one side like the one described above. Wagons loaded with tobacco were pulled alongside the building. Workers on the wagon would pass the sticks of tobacco through the hole to other workers who were strategically located on the ground or astraddle the tier poles inside the barn.

A Green County example, found near Exie, is composed of a single log pen which measures twenty-eight by twenty-eight by eighteen feet and is enclosed by twelve foot boxed sheds on all sides, thus making the total dimensions fifty-two by fifty-two feet. The sheds were added in 1872. The logs are generally very large; one measures fourteen inches by nineteen feet. Saddle notching was employed.

An old log double-pen barn, built in 1860, is located two miles north of Columbia near the banks of Russell Creek (Fig. 34). It has a side-to-side driveway after the fashion of the English hay barn, and there are doors leading from the driveway into the log pens. These features indicate an initial function as a livestock barn; but this structure was apparently erected as a tobacco barn, for there is a log weight-bearing wall in each pen which begins about four feet above the ground. Tobacco workers could pass readily beneath the low log. This particular barn is the only known one of its kind. It probably is not a relic of a vanished barn type, but is a mutant which its builder, James P. Murray, devised by drawing upon construction ideas from the more common types of the pre-Civil War period.

The dark tobacco belt of western Kentucky is characterized by a barn which presents a narrow profile on the landscape (Fig. 35). Its narrowness causes the entire structure to appear to have a more than normal height. The tall, narrow appearance is diminished somewhat by the addition of wing sheds. These barns are used in the fire-curing process necessary in the production of dark tobacco.

Figure 31. Cow barn. Log cow barns like this central Kentucky example have given way to framed examples of similar form which serve as dairy barns.

Figure 32. Typical tobacco barn. Note the ventilator which extends the full distance along the ridgeline of the roof. Photographed in westcentral Kentucky.

Figure 33. Tobacco barn photographed in central Kentucky.

Figure 34. Log double-pen tobacco barn, built in Adair County in 1860.

Figure 35. Dark tobacco barn. Extremely tall, slender barns are typical of the dark tobacco belt of western Kentucky. These structures are essentially airtight, so that heat may be retained during the fire curing process. Photographed near the Tidewater River.

Epilogue

FOLK HOUSES, house construction, cribs, and barns comprise only a portion of the broader field of folk architecture. For example, no mention was made in this study of the smaller outbuildings that are components of the totality of the farmstead, such as cellars, ice houses, smokehouses, and privies.

There is an entire new field of study known to folklorists as folklife or folk material culture studies. This field is concerned with the visible and artifactual aspects of folk behavior that existed prior to and concurrently with mechanized industry. Folklife studies are concerned with the skills, techniques, and traditional formulas transmitted across the years by persons and cultures that prize cultural stability above social change. There is a pressing need, in the words of Richard M. Dorson in *Folklore and Folklife: An Introduction* (University of Chicago, 1972), to know more about "how men and women in tradition-oriented societies build their homes, make their clothes, prepare their food, farm and fish, process the earth's bounty, fashion their tools and implements, and design their furniture and utensils. . ." (pp. 2–3).

It is hoped that this small volume will serve as a stimulus to Kentuckians who desire to know more of their folk heritage. As we earlier stated, this work may profitably be utilized as a handbook of folk house and barn types across the commonwealth. All the common varieties of structures are included here. The less common types and the many mutated forms are not included, however. Individual studies of these and other aspects of Kentucky's material culture are sorely needed.

When possible and practicable we wrote in the present tense. Many of the structures pictured and described were still existent on the culture landscape when this work was begun in 1963. Regrettably, such is no longer the case. At least two-fifths of these priceless old structures have disappeared within the past decade, due either to the ravages of time or to the often destructive needs of society. We urge all readers to seek out, to map, to photograph, and to do measured drawings of folk buildings, and to interview persons who still recall something of the history of these structures and the people who occupied them or used them.

House and Barn Plans

Central Passage Houses

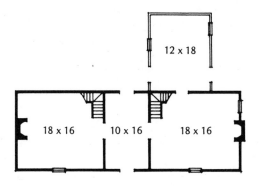

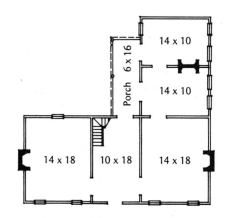

Frame Construction
Log Construction

Dog Trot Houses

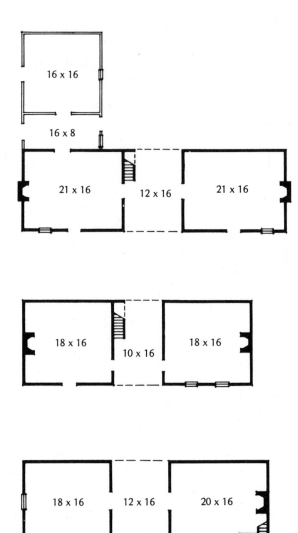

Saddlebag Houses

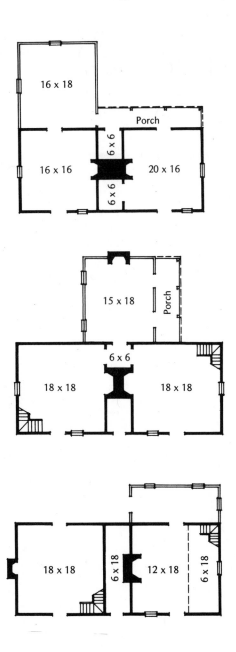

I Houses

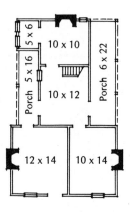

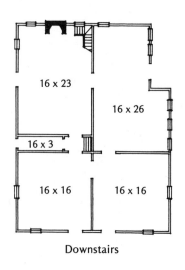

Downstairs

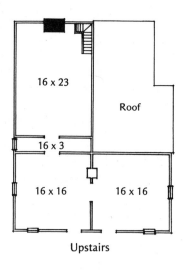

Upstairs

I Houses

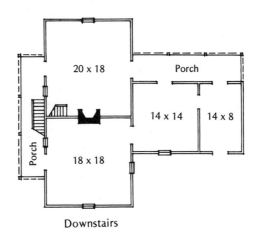

Downstairs

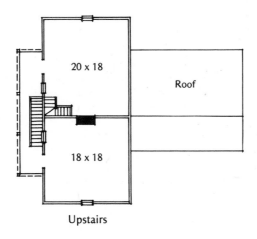

Upstairs

I Houses

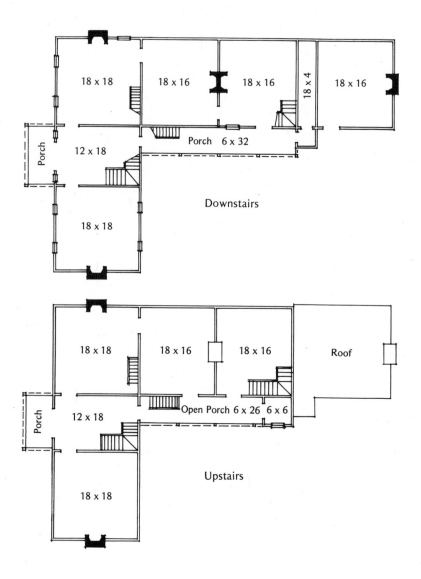

18 x 18 18 x 16 18 x 16 18 x 4 18 x 16

Porch

Porch   6 x 32

12 x 18

Downstairs

18 x 18

18 x 18 18 x 16 18 x 16 Roof

Porch

12 x 18

Open Porch 6 x 26 6 x 6

Upstairs

18 x 18

Varieties of Cribs

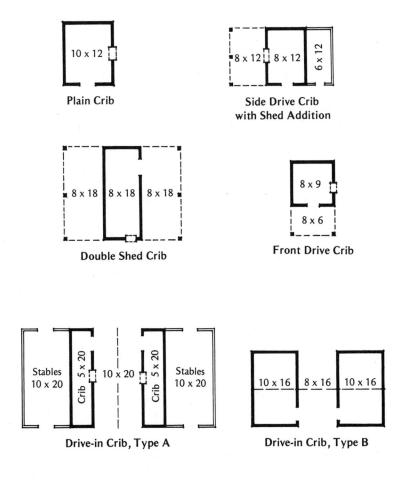

10 x 12

Plain Crib

8 x 12 | 8 x 12 | 6 x 12

**Side Drive Crib
with Shed Addition**

8 x 18 | 8 x 18 | 8 x 18

Double Shed Crib

8 x 9

8 x 6

Front Drive Crib

Stables
10 x 20 | Crib 5 x 20 | 10 x 20 | Crib 5 x 20 | Stables
10 x 20

Drive-in Crib, Type A

10 x 16 | 8 x 16 | 10 x 16

Drive-in Crib, Type B

— — — — Ridge of Roof

☐ Grain Windows

Double Crib Barn

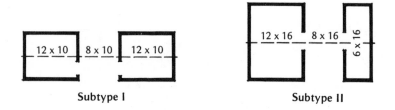

12 x 10   8 x 10   12 x 10

Subtype I

12 x 16   8 x 16   6 x 16

Subtype II

Single Crib Barns

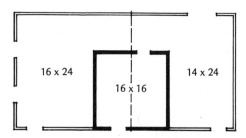

16 x 24   14 x 24

16 x 16

**Log Barn with Shed
Additions on Three Sides**

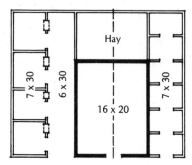

Hay

7 x 30   6 x 30   7 x 30

16 x 20

**Log Barn with Hay Bin,
Drive & Stabling Areas**

Evolution of Four Crib Barn to
a Transverse Crib Barn

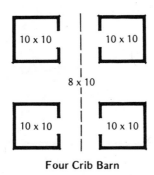

10 x 10	10 x 10

8 x 10

10 x 10	10 x 10

Four Crib Barn

Tobacco
28 x 9

Tobacco

- - - - - - - - - -

Stable 10 x 9	8 x 9	Stable 10 x 9

Lower Level

Hay	Hay & Corn	Hay

Upper Level

Transverse Crib Barns

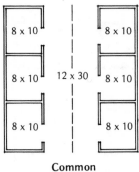

Common

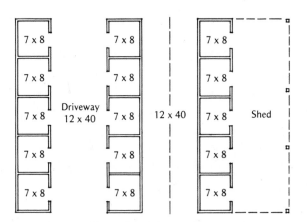

**Large Stock Barn Subtype with
Two Driveways & Shed Addition**

English Barns

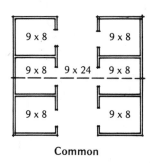

Common

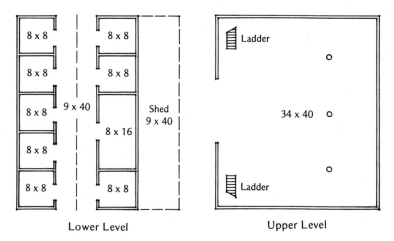

Lower Level   Upper Level

Bank Barn Subtype

Notes to the Reader

Numerous excellent studies of folk architecture have been published in Europe. Articles in the English language have appeared regularly in the journals *Folk-Liv, Gwerin, Folk Life, Ulster Folklife,* and *Scottish Studies.* Few seminal works on folk dwellings have yet been produced in America, and the bulk of these were done by cultural geographers. Fred Kniffen, professor emeritus at Louisiana State University, showed the way with "Louisiana House Types," in *Annals of the Association of American Geographers* 26 (1936), 179–93. Kniffen's "Folk Housing: Key to Diffusion," *Annals of the Association of American Geographers* 55 (1965), 549–77, which is a good survey of folk architecture in the eastern United States, also does much to reveal why cultural geographers have done far more research on folk architecture than folklorists have. Other geographers whose works contributed to our present study include Richard Pillsbury and Andrew Kardos, *A Field Guide to the Folk Architecture of the Northeastern United States* (Dartmouth, N.H.: Dartmouth College, 1970); Eugene M. Wilson, "The Single Pen Log House in the South," *Pioneer America* 2 (1970), 21–28, and "Some Similarities between American and European Folk Houses," *Pioneer America* 3 (1971), 8–13; John Fraser Hart and Eugene Cotton Mather, "The Character of Tobacco Barns and Their Role in the Tobacco Economy of the United States," *Annals of the Association of American Geographers* 51 (1961), 288–93; and Wilbur Zelinsky, "The Log House in Georgia," *The Geographical Review* 43 (1953), 173–86.

All of the foregoing studies stress form as the basic

criterion for understanding the nature of folk housing. Amos Rapoport, in *House Form and Culture* (New York: Prentice-Hall, 1969), seeks to understand how house form occurs. He proposes a challenging conceptual interdisciplinary framework for looking at the great variety of world house types and forms and the forces that affect them.

Warren E. Roberts, Indiana University folklorist, wrote a chapter on "Folk Architecture," for Richard M. Dorson's *Folklore and Folklife: An Introduction* (Chicago: University of Chicago Press, 1972). Folklorists look mainly to Henry Glassie, a folklife specialist at Indiana University, for leadership in the area of folk architectural studies, however. Glassie's studies were utilized heavily in the preparation of the present study, and we hereby acknowledge our debt to him. While his basic theories are set forth in *Pattern in the Material Folk Culture of the Eastern United States* (Philadelphia: University of Pennsylvania, 1969), the student of folk architecture will need to dig into Glassie's extensive periodical publications for more detailed information on the various building types, their origins and patterns of distribution. See, e.g., "Southern Mountain Houses: A Study in American Folk Culture," Master's Thesis, American Folk Culture Program, Cooperstown, New York, 1965; "The Appalachian Log Cabin," *Mountain Life and Work* 39 (1963), 5–14; "The Old Barns of Appalachia," *Mountain Life and Work* 40 (1965), 21–30; "The Pennsylvania Barn in the South," *Pennsylvania Folklife* 15 (1965–66), 8–19, and 16 (1966), 12–25; "The Double-Crib Barn in South Central Pennsylvania," *Pioneer America* 1:1 (1969), 9–16; 1:2 (1969), 40–45; 2:1 (1970), 47–52; 2:2 (1970), 23–34.

Students of folk architecture will find much valuable and interesting information, especially about exterior and interior design, in the publications of architectural historians. We have drawn upon the following sources for data: Henry Chandlee Forman, *The Architecture of the Old South: The Medieval Period, 1585–1850* (New York: Russell and Russell, 1948); Fiske Kimball, *Domestic Architecture of the American Colonies and of the Early Republic* (New York: C. Scribner's Sons, 1927); Talbot F. Hamlin, *Greek Revival Architecture in America* (New York: Dover Publications, 1964); John Mead Howells, *Lost Examples of Colonial Architecture*, reprint, (New York: Dover Publications, 1963); Norman M. Isham and Albert F. Brown, *Early Connecticut Houses* (New York: Dover Publications, 1965); J. Frederick Kelly, *The Early Domestic Architecture of Connecticut* (New York: Dover Publications, 1963); Henry L. and Ottalie K. Williams, *A Guide to Old American Houses 1700-1900* (New York: Barnes, 1962) and *Old American Houses: How to Restore, Remodel and Reproduce Them* (New York: Coward-McCam, 1957). An important recent study of log buildings is Donald A. Hutsler's "The Log Architecture of Ohio," *Ohio History* (1971), 172–271.

For information on Kentucky architecture, mainly distinguished architecture, see: J. Winston Coleman, Jr., *Old Homes of the Blue Grass* (Lexington: Kentucky Society, 1950); Thomas A. Knight and Nancy L. Greene, *Country Estates of the Blue Grass* (Cleveland: Britton Publishing Company, 1904); Rexford Newcomb, *Architecture in Old Kentucky* (Urbana, Ill.: University of Illinois, 1953) and *Old Kentucky Architecture* (New York: W. Helburn, Inc., 1940); Elizabeth M. Simpson, *Bluegrass Houses and Their Traditions* (Lexington: Transylvania Press, 1932); and Elizabeth P. Thomas, *Old Kentucky Homes and Gardens* (Louisville: Standard Printing Company, 1939). A splendid article entitled "The Log Houses of Kentucky," by James C. Thomas, appeared in *Antiques* (1974), 791–98. Much valuable information can also be gleaned from Emmet F. Horine, ed., *Pioneer Life in Kentucky 1785–1800 by Daniel Drake, M.D.* (New York: Henry Shuman, 1948).

Barns appear in some of the publications already cited. The student of barns may also wish to consult the following: Charles H. Dornbusch and John K. Heyl, *Penn-*

sylvania German Barns, Pennsylvania German *Folklore Society* 21 (Allentown, Pa.: Schlechter's, 1958); Alfred L. Shoemaker et al., *The Pennsylvania Barn* (Lancaster: Pennsylvania Dutch Folklore Center, 1955), which stresses various aspects of construction and design of Pennsylvania barns; Eric Sloane, *American Barns and Covered Bridges* (New York: Wilfred Funk, Inc., 1954), which discusses different features and accessories of American barns, and *An Age of Barns* (New York: Funk and Wagnalls, 1966), a work devoted to interior structuring, tools used to make barns, and barn types.

For an excellent but dated commentary on the origin of log construction in Europe and America, consult Harold R. Shurtleff, *The Log Cabin Myth* (Cambridge: Harvard University Press, 1939); see also Hugh Morrison, *Early American Architecture from the First Colonial Settlements to the National Period* (New York: Oxford University Press, 1952), and Kniffen and Glassie, "Building in Wood in the Eastern United States: A Time-Place Perspective," *The Geographical Review* 56 (1966), 40–66.

Log end notching is one of the most distinguishing constructional aspects of the American log house. A fine beginning point for the reader is Fred Kniffen, "On Corner-Timbering," *Pioneer America* 1 (1969), 1–8. See also Kniffen and Glassie, "Building in Wood . . . ," 48–57.

For brief descriptions of log interstice chinking, see Wight H. Marshall, "The 'Thousand Acre' Log House, Monroe County, Indiana," *Pioneer America* 3 (1971), 48–56; William J. Murtagh, "Half Timbering in American Architecture," *Pennsylvania Folklife* 8 (1958), 3–11; Peter O. Wacker and Roger T. Tindell, "The Log House in New Jersey," *Keystone Folklore Quarterly* 13 (1968), 248–68; and Wilson, "The Single Pen Log House in the South."

Roofing methods and materials are described by, among numerous others, Bradford Angier, "Shake Roof," *The Beaver,* Outfit 293 (1945), 52–53; Gösta Berg, "The

Sawing by Hand of Boards and Planks," *Folk-Liv* (1957–58), 1–11; and Eliot Wigginton, ed., *The Foxfire Book* (Garden City, New York: Doubleday, 1972), 45–52.

Porches and rear and gable end additions to houses are generally overlooked by scholars. Henry Glassie offers a beginning point in "The Types of the Southern Mountain Cabin," in Jan Brunvand, *The Study of American Folklore* (New York: W. W. Norton and Company, 1968). Perhaps more rewarding sources of information are autobiographies and personal accounts of folklife; e.g., Tate C. Page, "The Voices of Moccasin Creek," 423 pp. unpublished manuscript, 1972, on file in the Helm Library at Western Kentucky University. This is the most complete description of frontier life that we have been privileged to read.